Unto His Glory

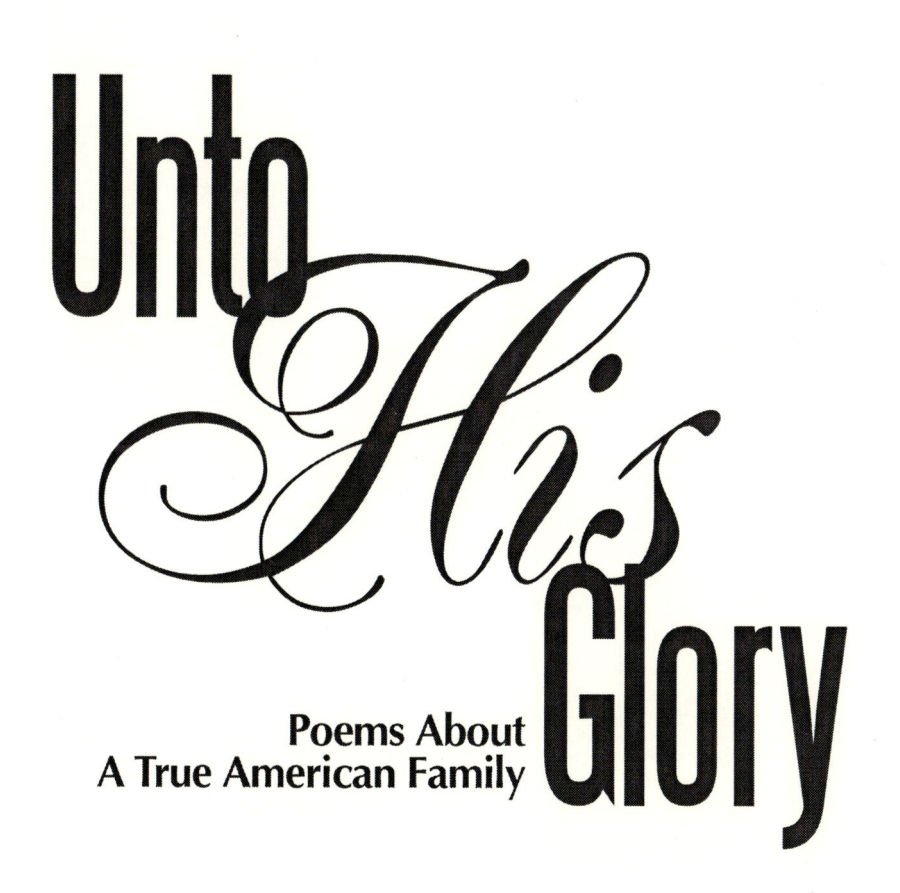

Poems About A True American Family

Patricia Swain

UNTO HIS GLORY
Copyright © 2009 by Patricia Swain

All Rights Reserved under International Copyright Law.
Contents and/or cover may not be reproduced in any form,
stored in a retrieval system or transmitted
in any form by any means –
electronic, mechanical, photocopy, recording or otherwise –
without prior written permission of the publisher.

ISBN 978-0-9817603-2-2

Published by:
Seed Word Communications
P.O. Box 16615
Tallahassee, FL 32317
USA: +1.850.765.0386
www.seedword.com

Cover Design by Ruth Palao: www.rpvdesigns.com
Page Design by Nancy Apple: www.designingapple.com

DEDICATIONS

I dedicate this book to my husband, my children, step-children, grand children, and great-grand children. I also dedicate it to all my brothers and sisters, nieces, nephew and all my cousins of many different generations. Finally, I dedicate this book to the memory of my grandparents, my parents, aunts, uncles, brother, sister and nephew, all of who have gone on to heaven ahead of the rest of the family.

FOREWORD

by Joan Copps

The heart is a hiding place for many thoughts, actions and secrets. Good singers sing from the heart. Many writers also write from the heart. From the abundance of the heart, the mouth speaks.

"Unto His Glory" has been written from Patricia Swain's heart. Her writings stem from a young girl's dreams and wishes, until now, a mother's and grandmother's joys are seen manifested.

Her faith in Christ has not altered since her childhood teachings. There is a tendency to bring up our children in the ways we were raised. Her standards and banner, she holds high and dear to her teachings.

Life's experiences are expressed in her poetry. Her family, near and far, is precious to her as you will realize in her poetic form.

Having known Pat for nearly thirty years, His Glory has been evident in her life.

May you be blessed, as you enjoy her writing "Unto His Glory."

CONTENTS

DEDICATIONS iii
FOREWORD iv

SECTION ONE 1
   Unto His Glory 2
   My Guardian Angel Went Home 4
   Loose Him, And Let Him Go 9
   I'll See You 13
   Golden Years 20
   In Memory 32
   You Can Come Home Now 36
   Stand Up For A Lady 41
   Modern Romance 43
   Tricia's Romance 45
   Dear Wanda 49
   My Daddy 51
   Family Reunion 53
   Please Don't Unravel My Brain 56
   Our Christmas Together 58
   A Note To Woody 61
   Through The Garden Gate 62
   Please Send Jesus 64

Have A Party 65
Daniel 68
Will T. Bear 70
Erica 72
Only God 74
It's Ok To Ask Why 75
Hi Daddy 78

SECTION TWO 81
How About It, Kids? 82
What If? 84
Ode Of A Lost Birthday Card 87
Zip It, If You Must 90
Who Do We Appreciate? 92
Class Of '58 97
Project Turnaround 99
Quiet Night 102
What A Pastor Is Like 104
Just In Case You Didn't Know 106
They Pierced My Sides, Too 109
What Is It Like To Be Fifty? 112
Happy Children's Day 114
How To Keep From Getting Old 116
Happy 53rd 118

Happy Birthday 121
Just To Prove It 123
You Know I Will 126
A View From The Pew 128
What Makes a Good Family Reunion? 130
Writing 133
All In A Pastor's Day 134

SECTION THREE 138
Just Wondering 139
God's Footstool 142
Finishing Touch 143
How To Remodel Your House 145
Will You Cast Me Aside, Lord? 148
What Mama Knew 152
Time Goes On 157
Computers 159
'Twas The Day After Thanksgiving 161
The ABC's Of Living 163
How Will It Be? 165
Forever Spring 167
Time Goes On 169
I Need A Valentine 171
Holiday Woes 173
I Am Sixty-Three 175

SECTION FOUR 177

'Twas Two Weeks Before Christmas 178
The Way To Eternal Happiness 181
He'll Be There 183
Right On Time 185
What If He Did It Again 187
The Year Of Ninety-Eight 188
Stand Up For Jesus 190
You Don't Have To Wait For Heaven 192
If You Have A Light, Just Let It Shine 194
Songs We Love 196
For Such A Time As This 198
There Are No Heartaches 200
Please Don't Ask Me To Be Still 201
The Older Brother And Judas 202
What Would They Say 204
What Is Your Idol? 206
Let Not Your Heart Be Troubled 208
Could We Find Room For Him? 210
Gabriel Has The Trumpet Ready 213

SECTION ONE

Section one is made up of twenty-five poems. Each poem is written about a family member, or a friend of some family member. They were written over a lifetime. Sometimes, I was sad, while at other times happy. Before each of the poems, I give the reason it is written.

I am confident that you will enjoy reading this book of poetry because I have put my heart in these pages. Sometimes, the tears came instead of words. At those times, God washed away hurt, for awhile.

This first little poem was written last. It was not written until I decided the title for this book. While I was eating breakfast on Tuesday, March 13, 2007, I took a New Testament out of my pocket, and wrote my name in it and also wrote the words, "Unto His Glory." I immediately knew that was going to be the title of this book.

Unto His Glory

Unto His Glory, was this book written
Unto His Glory, may it also be read
May you always find me writing
Until the day, you find me dead.

Well, allow me to restate this
There will be an eternity
Where all will be for His Glory
So, maybe He chose writing for me.

Now, how do you really know
I won't be writing all those songs
The saints will be eternally singing
Of how Jesus forgave their wrongs?

There is one thing, I know for sure
We will need a lot of books
When Charity gets to heaven
For what else will she look?

Someone will have to write instructions
So the mansions will be spic and span
To Teresa, who is always cleaning
Follow my instructions, if you can

What makes you think, ain't so?
That we won't need anyone to write?
We will have a lot of things to do
Where there will be no night.

We'll also need a cookbook
For those who have been selected
To cook all that wonderful food
As the cookbook has directed.

You may think I am dreaming
Or, you may know I am crazy
But there is one thing for sure
No writer has ever been lazy.

So leave me alone, let me be
God will give me a golden pen
I'll write it all, "Unto His Glory"
Over and over, and over again.

March 13, 2007

My Guardian Angel Went Home

This poem was written right after the death of my mother, Frances Gladys Proffitt Abram, on June 15, 1999. She was sick for a long time. For the most of her last year, she was taken care of as if she were a baby. I was not prepared for the day she died, even though I knew death was coming.

It took about two weeks to write this poem, because the words would not come that truly expressed my feelings. It was only a couple of weeks after her death that I also got sick. After that, something happened to me. I never really knew what was wrong. I was sent to a neurologist and had a lot of tests performed on me. Although, with symptoms of various physical ailments, all the tests proved negative

I couldn't cope with anyone touching me, especially my arms and legs. For that reason, I turned the couch into my bed. I didn't sleep very well either. I couldn't even stand hearing my husband's voice.

By the time we had family reunion in August 2001, I was unable to attend, because I couldn't drive from Florida to West Virginia. Through much prayer, I finally was my old self again. Actually, God healed my spirit.

How many times, did I hear someone say
Mama won't be with us many more days?
Rapidly, her health seemed to be declining
Earth, no longer, seemed to hold a binding.

Mama, your eyes had that gaze, far away
Like you were seeing, yet another day
Where neither eyes have seen, nor ears heard
What God has prepared, as He says in His Word.

The times Mama, when you were so very ill
It seemed you stayed here, only by your will
I know the God you loved so much
Each day now, I feel his gentle touch.

I am not crying because you went home
I just feel you left me here, so all alone
Then, I remember, and quickly dry my eyes
You are at home Mama, just beyond the skies.

I remember the day so very well
June 15, Alicia called me just to tell
Mama left us earlier today
I had to guess the news, she could not say.

Mama, I knew the time was close at hand
When God would welcome you to yonder land
But, I didn't think it would be this soon
I planned to see you following Friday at noon.

Now, I wanted to get home as fast as I could
Although a little rest, I knew I should
But, Mama, you are doing the resting now
I just wanted to get to you somehow.

Soon, my tears were gone, I couldn't feel
It didn't seem like the news was real
When I walked in to fix your hair
I realized, it was really you lying there.

Mama, your hair was so long, and thin
Could I make it look the way it was, again?
It seemed, that angels were standing all around
A new courage, and strength, I found.

Mama, as I looked at you lying, cold and still.
I thought, Lord, surely you know I will
Use that determination, I see on your face
To take me also to that glorious place.

You wanted to lay in the church overnight
I felt this was most certainly all right
The church, where you attended nearly fifty years
The place, where you had shed a million tears.

Tears of sadness, tears of pure joy
As you, so often prayed, for each girl and boy
Sixty-two years, you had served the Lord
Now, it was time for your reward.

Your funeral was carried out, as you planned
A red rose was placed in each child's hand
The rose said "Pat, I love you"
"Mama," I cried, "I love you too."

As Kenneth preached your funeral, I recall
He spoke to your children, one and all
Mama is home, where she desired to be
To see her again, is up to you, and to me.

A soldier in the Lord's army, you had been
You proved it, over and over again
The Christian Flag was placed over you
A symbol, that to God, you had been true.

Mama, as your funeral came to a close
All the congregation then arose
"What A Mighty God, We Serve" rang out
You were singing too, I have no doubt.

Now Mama, I was there through it all
I talk about you, and try to recall
But, Mama, you are not gone anywhere
In my heart, I have you, very near.

Nothing seems real, though I know it's so
I am not able, to really let you go
I look at your picture, I shake my head
You can't tell me, that Mama is dead.

She is just visiting, in another land
Probably rejoicing with the angel band
As, she awaits, our arrival there
To join her, in a land free of care.

Family reunion, will never be the same
Unless I pretend I hear you call my name
You will always be there, if just for me
As I close my eyes, your face I can see.

Mama, I am always thinking, of something to say
Then I remember, Oh, yes, she is away
But, as sure as God, sits on his throne
One day soon, they will count me gone.

Gone to where, there are no more tears
Gone to a place, where there are no fears
Basking in His eternal love
Mama, I'll see you soon, in that home above.

You were the one who taught me of Him
My vision of Calvary has never grown dim
Because of you Mama, I'll see His face
And thank Him for that Amazing Grace.

July 23, and July 29, 1999

Loose Him, And Let Him Go

On December 2, 1988, I received a call, while at work. It was from Mom. She told me Daddy passed away that morning. I knew, he had been sick for a long time. He was a diabetic. He was nearly blind, could barely speak loud enough for me to hear him, and could hardly hear what I said to him. I suppose you would say he was lonely in a house full of people because of the difficult time we had communicating with him.

He also had black lung, a disease associated with working all those years in the coal mines. It was hard for him to breathe. He used a fan on him as he slept summer and winter. My children picked up that habit, and to this day, summer or winter, they each have a fan, blowing full force. Their spouses crawl deeper under the covers.

This next poem was written a week after Daddy died. The scripture this poem is based on is St. John 11: 44. I did not understand the full meaning, until after I returned home from his funeral. It gave me a clearer understanding of death.

> The Lord gave me a sermon
> A few days before Daddy died
> I wrote the message down
> Then, just set it aside.
>
> I was going to deliver it
> When the right time came
> I felt the message came from God
> I still feel the same.

St. John, eleventh chapter, verse forty-four
Is where the text is found.
"When Jesus came to Bethany,
Grief of death had Martha and Mary bound…"

Jesus wept. Not for the dead
But for those who were living
As their brother lay asleep
And in their hearts, they were grieving.

They could not see beyond the grave
To where the saints are gone
They thought that he was dead
While life was still going on.

Jesus felt their heavy burden
Just as He feels yours and mine
If we could only see beyond the grave
And know His plans divine.

Jesus said "If thou would just believe
Thou should surely see, God's glory"
I say the same for us today
This is not a new kind of story.

They stood there at the grave
As Jesus stood there too
Can't help but to realize
They were like me and you.

Jesus always has it under control
Just as he did on that day
When he spoke to the people
To take the big stone away.

As he spoke "Lazarus, come forth"
Death had to release his hold
Lazarus came from the tomb
Just as he was told.

He was bound in grave clothes
Couldn't see him, you know
Until Jesus, told the crowd
Loose him and let him go.

I thought about this message
When Daddy passed away
How God performs His wonders
Just as then, the same today.

My Daddy too was unable to see
He could not freely hear
Just as for Lazarus then
Jesus knew and came near.

I hope people will understand
What I am trying to say
The Death Angel loosed Daddy
And let him walk away.

He was bound with blindness
His body ached with pain
His speech was, low, his hearing gone
Health, he would never regain.

December second, he got his healing
When Jesus came to his side
How would you like to go home
There, forever you will abide?

He is loose, and he is free
To run over the streets, of gold
There in his eternal home
He will never grow old.

Now, I want to ask you
"Does sin have you bound?
Do you find you're always running
Knowing, Satan has you down?"

If you are bound with sin
Jesus will come to you, I know
If you will ask Him, He will say
"Satan, loose him and let him go."

December 9, 1988

I'll See You

I knew Daddy was not well, that he was a diabetic and had a lot of medical problems. But, the words, "Your Daddy passed away this morning," seemed like a cruel joke. Couldn't possibly tell you how I really felt inside, but will try in the following poem, written just for Daddy.

Well, Daddy, guess I'll talk to you awhile
Try to tell you how I feel
Never dreamed, when I saw you last
Next time, you would be so still.

Mom called me, December second
Same day you had to go
She told me, "Do not worry
Your Daddy made it home, I know".

Well, Daddy, I haven't the words to tell you
The way I really felt that day
When I realized what Mom had said
I didn't have mind enough to pray.

Soon it became just like a dream
Everything seemed so far away
As I planned, and packed our things
I couldn't find any words to say.

I wanted to get home to Mom
As I drove mile after mile
I got lost so many times
I couldn't help but smile.

I thought my mind was playing tricks
Or maybe I had it trained well
To do what I want it to do
Of bad things not to tell

I wondered what it would be like
As I turned into your driveway
Then suddenly I realized
Daddy's not in the porch swing today.

What had seemed like a dream
Had suddenly become quite real
I could hardly move myself
Could barely walk, or feel.

Then Mom came and hugged me
To tell me you are better now
No need to cry and grieve so much
Please, someone just tell me how.

Then I thought, how selfish of me
To even wish that you were here
Nothing in this life can compare
To what, I visualize, you have up there.

Daddy, you really have it made
You and Randy, there together too
Rejoicing around the throne of God
Guess I really envy the two of you.

Teresa and Duane weren't able to stay
To be with the family Sunday night
They went to see you earlier
Mr. Bailey said it was all right.

I went with them for the viewing
Thought I had it under control
Daddy, I did. I really did
I felt really brave and bold.

I walked into the cold chapel
Daddy, Oh, Daddy, there you lay
I tried, but couldn't touch you, Daddy
Some force seemed to pull my hand away.

I wondered why I had to feel like this
When your wishes had been filled
As the cold hand of the Death Angel
Your tired body, he gently stilled.

We all came back that night
Together we cried and cried
Friends came by the hundreds
As they stood by our sides.

You left twelve of us kids
Each one special in our own way
Together we gave you twenty-nine grands
Plenty enough, wouldn't you say?

The grandchildren took up the pace
Supplying you with ten great
Two more on the way, you know
The world they try to populate.

The older grandsons carried you, Daddy
I thought that was truly good
The many times you carried their cares
Making them as happy as you could.

Daddy, I stood over alone
As I talked to you that night
I told you how glad I was for you
I knew, up there, you were all right.

I thought of how you had suffered
You couldn't hear, you couldn't see
You were very lonely among us
To want you back, so selfish of me.

Mom said you left so easy
Never once felt any pain
She said you have it made now
Our loss is just heaven's gain.

The last time I talked with you, Daddy
We talked a lot about our leaving
When our time should come to go
And our rewards we'd be receiving.

I was all smiles, thinking of that home
Knowing you were just waiting to go
Death seemed a long way off then
How was I to really know?

I was planning to see you, Daddy
When we had a family reunion again
I'd sit down in the swing with you
As you'd ask, "How have you been?"

Family reunions won't be quite the same
As the swing sits empty and still
We have to once again remind ourselves
Yes, children, it is really real.

Oh, let me tell you, Daddy
Before I have to go
How your funeral took place
As if you don't already know.

The starting time was set for one
The family all came real early
We had to have more time with you
Each moment we had, we held dearly.

The organ played softly, as time drew near
Then, for a while, time just stood still
When they gently closed your casket
I thought, this can't be real.

They started singing, "I Won't Have to Worry"
I thought, Daddy, how very true for you
Next, they sang, "Until Then"
How appropriate this song was too.

Brother Sibble spoke briefly to all of us
Of how you desired to go
Then Brother Shewsbury read the list of survivors
Took a little time, as you know.

We heard a tape by Kenneth and Brenda
As they sang, "I Firmly Promise You"
Daddy, I don't remember their first song
But, somehow, I think you do.

Kenneth preached your funeral, Daddy
As you had asked him to
Really, he was just the instrument
The message came from you.

The chapel seemed so hazy
The Spirit of God was so strong
I thought, we'll soon be with you
I know it can't be long.

You had beautiful flowers
Seven sprays were from Churches of God
Representing the different churches
Your children's feet had trod.

The flowers my church sent
Seemed to speak to me
Saying, "They are with you now
As you would like them to be."

Then, Daddy, they were asking us to stand
So one by one we could pass by
To take the final earthly view
And wait for our time to fly.

To a world unknown to mortal man
Where time will know no end
Beneath the burden of our grief
The body never has to bend.

I walked up to you Daddy
I looked at your pale face
Knowing death had claimed you
But you live in a better place.

I didn't want to say good-bye
Just didn't seem the thing to do
Then, I bent and kissed your cheek
And, whispered, "I promise I'll see you."

December 7, 1988

Golden Years

On November 4, 1985, Mom and Dad had been married for 50 years. Of course, we had a big celebration for them. If you know anything about me, you know I had to write a poem for the occasion. In one part of the program, I read the poem, and as I read about each of their children, the person came forward and stood behind Mom and Dad. When I got to the grand children, they all came up and took their place with the rest of the family.

This poem was written in one day, because as I got started, I just couldn't stop until it was finished.

November, yes it was the 4th
The year was nineteen hundred thirty five
Post depression years, if you please
Most souls thankful just to survive.

There was one young man, very spry
Walked himself daily, miles and miles
To see a young lady, just barely fifteen
She was the reason for his smiles.

This young lady was Ma's little baby
No wolf would get her Red Riding Hood
Look out Ma, Isaac has a plan
Gonna be my wife, I know you understood.

ELOPE, I guess that's what you call it
Ma called this deal stealing
But, who couldn't steal a wife
When Gladys was quite willing?

Would take a book to write their story
But a few high points I will give you
Telling of the bad times, and the good
Always, there was something new.

The first New baby was born February, tenth
The year, still post depression, thirty seven
He enriched this meager home
Just as dough is with leaven.

James Randolph became his name
Randy was what we called him
Always full of adventures
Till evening shadows grew dim.

Remember that old ground hog
Randy saw early one morning?
He stuck his head out of the hole, and said
"Good morning, little boy" without a warning.

The day he became a Christian
I remember very well
When he came into the room
A difference I could tell.

Time has a way of moving
And changing things you see
On November 22nd, the year thirty eight
Mercy, what might this be.

You guessed it, a little girl
Wanda Louise became her tag
One thing certain, she didn't know
She had no time to lag.

She was barely steady on her feet, when
what to their wondering eyes should appear
Too early for the Easter bunny
Too late for Santa's reindeer.

Yeah, you guessed it again
February 26, forty was the year
Another little baby girl
I guess, she was held dear.

As war planes were designed
Life seemed full of uncertainties
All had to take second place
Now, "What shall the baby's name be?"

Thinking and thinking and trying real hard
Patience must have been put to a test
Patricia Ann was agreed upon
Just plain Pat is the rest.

She was called Patsy and Patty
Her grandma called her Patty Go
Because, when the car moved out of sight
Where was Patty? You should know.

Bonnie June was next in line
No one seemed the least surprised
A girl every year, or two
It seemed, everyone realized.

Bonnie was born on March 5
Still war years of nineteen, forty-two
When little sister gets bigger
I'll see what I can teach you.

Teach her, you just believe it
Whatever the adventures might be
Bonnie would be in the same trouble
To this, I was going to see.

We climbed the cherry tree
Something we were not allowed to do
When we saw Mom with a switch
Don't you cry girl, I dare you.

We played like we were movie stars
Wrote and put on our shows
Did a lot of make believe
What all else, only heaven knows.

Life went on in those McDowell hills
Daddy was a coal miner you see
With all us "younguns" yelling
Mom stayed as busy as a bee.

Did you think I had forgotten
To tell about the next baby?
I wouldn't do you that way
Oh, well, yes just maybe.

Why don't you try to guess?
What do you think she was?
A little girl, of course
Nothing cries as loud as a girl does.

It was now the year nineteen forty three
On the fifteenth day of June
Velma Elizabeth did surely arrive
Maybe, you think it was too soon.

Regardless of what you think
Or, what anyone may say
The next one was even closer
Guess it is better that way.

You don't have to learn to wash diapers
When you already know how
So bring on those Indians
And have a big pow wow.

What was the next one?
Well, now let's just see
One boy and four girls already
What should this one be?

To be or not to be
Another little squalling girl
Demanding all the attention
Taking her place in this our world.

August fourteen, year of forty-four
Evelyn Delores made her appearance
If you have seen her temper
You know how I made an endurance.

Dee still owes me a watch
The one she broke from my arm
When Mom left me in charge
And I meant no harm.

I only meant that Dee would mind
If I had to see to it
Seeing to it I was doing
When she threw her little fit.

She broke my watch, my treasure
That was a very valuable one
My brother got for fourteen dollars
The numbers were made of little stones.

Mercer County didn't end the ordeal
As you have already guessed by now
Mom, not another girl again
Oh, yes, some way and somehow.

Norma Jean, we shall call her
Although, we called her many names
Norma John, Norma Johnson, Pee Wee
John Boy, just call and she came.

September seventeen, of the year forty-six
Norma appeared at our house from nowhere
We knew she didn't come from heaven
Cause they ain't got no brats up there.

They told us the stork brought babies
We thought this was all true
We were always looking up at the sky
To see what else was coming new.

It seemed the stork would never come
If we children were home and awake
He acted just like Santa Claus
So sneaking, for goodness sake.

If at first you don't succeed
Try, try and try again
Maybe the next time you will win
If wishing real hard you have been.

I guess wishes do come true
When you want a little boy
Since, Kenneth Ray came our way
And filled our home with joy.

It was late in the year forty-seven
December thirteen was the day
We girls had to step aside
For a boy, to make way.

Trying to feed eight children
On a coal miner's fee
Took a lot of scraping the bottom
And, a lot of plain make believe.

Time rolls on and waits for none
Although it may pass us by
Another, yes another girl
To you, I dare not lie.

Then came nineteen and fifty
Where, did time ever go?
Gone with the wind, I guess
How should I ever know?

July ninth, Barbara Ellen was here
Might have known it was another girl
Sure made a big difference
In my own little world.

I became her second mama
And, rock her I would
Until she was totally spoiled
I'd trade her if I could.

When I came home from school
There she was, screaming
If I thought I would get to play
I certainly was a dreaming.

Was a cold, cold twenty-ninth
Of December, nineteen fifty-one,
When Thelma Marie decided to join us
Although, girls, we needed none.

Christmas isn't much fun
When Mama doesn't feel well
Things would soon be back to normal
This I could certainly tell.

Time went on, the world went around
Randy joined the Marines
Mom cried, and cried some more
Didn't want him to go it seems.

Had to stop the crying real soon
Since another baby would be due
Seems he was to replace Randy
So Mom wouldn't be so blue

Clarence Eugene, I helped to name
Was born August fifteen, fifty-five
My, what a long year it was
I felt lucky to be alive.

Machines replaced the coal miners
While my Daddy was no young guy
Finding another job some place
Was as hard as trying to fly.

We sometimes were hungry
Went weeks with very meager
When offered a job at five dollars a week
Take it, I was quite eager.

Every little bit helps
When there aren't many little bits
Up and doing what you can
Better than to just sit.

Must rush along, more to tell
About the dirty dozen
Yes, that's what we became
As that stork, again came buzzing.

Wilma Lee, born February eighth
Nineteen fifty-seven, the year
Maybe this will be the end
And that old stork leave here.

Lo, and behold, once again
That old stork fluttered in
Leaving another little girl
This time I think we win.

June, seventeen, of the year fifty-eight
Debra Gale became the CABOOSE
When Mom caught the old stork
Clipped his wings and turned him loose.

No longer can that old stork fly
And bring all those babies by
To have to feed and clothe and change
Till you feel like you will die.

Mom may have gotten the old stork
But not the other twenty-nine
That brought all those grandchildren
Each was one of a kind.

Don't forget those great grands
That somehow slipped in
Well, let's just face it
That old stork is at it again!

Mom and Dad, I know you're happy
As you look over the years
You see all the good times
All the memories you hold dear.

Randy is not with us now
How I wish he could be
To help us celebrate this day
Of your Golden Anniversary.

Just maybe, God in His glory
Calls him to the golden gate
Swings it back and lets him see
The joy as we celebrate.

Life has not been at all in vain
As, your children you loved and raised
You taught us the ways of God
To His name be all the praise.

October 26, 1985

In Memory

My brother Randy (James Randolph) went on a hunting trip, New Years Day of 1976. He was to be gone two days. He told Ruby, his wife, he would meet her back at home at 6:00 in the evening of January, third day. She was there as planned, but he didn't show. After about three or four hours, she went to his parent's home, which was less than a mile away. This was the beginning of an ordeal, that seemed to take us into eternity.

They searched for him four days before his body was found at a rest area on I-64 in the state of Virginia. Because of the autopsy and the condition of his body, we were unable to view him. For me, that was so hard to accept. I wanted to see him again. But, he was a Christian, so one day I will see him and know him as he was known in this life.

When he had been dead twelve years, we spent a couple of days in the Colonial Motel at Athens Georgia. While Woody, my husband, Charity, my daughter, and Bobby Lee, my grandson, were watching TV, I got in my corner of the room and tuned them out, while I wrote the following poem.

> I thought, as I entered the New Year
> What doeth thou hold for me
> Thou morning, amid the Athens hills
> Where rains fell swiftly and free.

The Colonial, quiet, lovely, peaceful
The sun hast but hidden her face
The strength of His unseen hand
The unmerited favor of His Grace.

I think back, I quickly recall
This same day, twelve years ago
The anguish that lay ahead
Mere mortals, we could not know.

The line so thin, motions unseen
Life's sweetest moments to a living soul
Ready, his Lord to meet at face
Death seemed only too bold.

Days without end, silently they passed
Questions, only God can satisfy
Wonderful, oh gracious King
In Thee, our hope does lie.

He only went on a short journey
Two days and I will be home
Meet me there at six o'clock
When from the trip, I have come.

Six o'clock came, you were not there
What has delayed you, my brother?
Did someone hinder your hasty steps?
Or did you go with another?

We looked and searched for miles
Knowing you were not unfaithful
You worried not the ones you loved
We held to hope, to God were grateful.

Our third day of eternity
Seemingly, no place else to look
Together we waited for word
Helplessly, new courage we took.

We gathered near the church
Our prayers seemed so small
As to our God we cried
Please give an answer, we accept all.

We waited another eternity
The phone did nothing but ring
We grasped that piece of hope
That good news it might bring.

I remember, Oh God, I remember
When the word came, we dread
Randy's truck had been found and
Yes, Randy was really dead.

So they said, they didn't know
He was as alive as anyone
Beyond the mortal touch of man
Caressed in the arms of God's own son.

No words can speak for me
How the heart cried and bled
Although, no tears would come
The Master came instead.

I saw Him, as He came
In a robe, long and white
He stood at my mama's knees
To let her know, Randy is all right.

She didn't seem to realize
Jesus really was right there
But, I saw Him. I gained strength
My Lord, stayed real near.

Twelve years have passed now
No less is our heart's pain
It won't be long, my brother
We know, we shall see you, again.

January 1, 1988

You Can Come Home Now

I arrived home, from church on Sunday night, June 13, 1993, around ten o'clock. Debbie, my sister, called to let me know, Wanda, my oldest sister, had been taken to the hospital.

Only a little while later, she called again and told me, the doctor said to call the family in. You have to be kidding, I thought. But, just the same, the next morning, my daughter, Trish, and I headed for Princeton, West Virginia. We arrived twelve hours later. I was the last to arrive, of the eleven remaining children.

Wanda was in ICU. They said she would not know me, but I am certain she knew me. When I told her my name, she had tears rolling down her face. She was trying to talk and I told her to let me do the talking, because I could see that she couldn't form the words.

Not, long after I got there, she was moved to a room, where we could stay with her all the time. Norma and I stayed all night. She had seizures all night. I stayed there, day and night, all week. I was waiting for her to come out of the coma, and talk to me. She never did.

I had to go back to Florida on Saturday. Tuesday, June 22, Debbie, called again. All she said was, "You can come home now." I knew Wanda was gone, and really knew, before she called. I may have been in Florida, but my spirit was with Wanda.

<blockquote>
You can come home now
Was all Debbie said to me
When she called late that night
Letting me know that you are free.
</blockquote>

I knew when Death walked in
Though I was many miles away
I felt within my spirit
This would be your final day.

Yes, Wanda, you'd suffer no more
Cares of life no longer show on your face.
God, in all His tender mercy
Wrapped you in love and grace.

Death carried you away
On the twenty-second of June
When I left you, three days before
I didn't know it would be this soon.

I guess I knew within
Hoping somehow I was wrong
Yet, when the phone rang
I knew you were gone.

Really, you were not gone
You had only answered the call
You can come home now
The words eventually come to all.

I drove the long miles back
To face what lurked ahead
I fought back the idea
That you could be dead.

I recalled the five days past
While, in silence you remained
I spoke your name, rubbed your arms
But consciousness, you never regained.

The closer I got to home
The more I felt reality
Not knowing, the real anguish
That would soon surround me.

In my mind, I saw the pink dress
You would be wearing that night
As you lay there before me
So peaceful, and so quiet.

When it was time to go in
The cold room, where you were
It was so hard to just look,
At you restfully, lying there.

I am not one to cry
And let my emotions show
My tears, I could not contain
I had to allow them to flow.

I looked at your flowers
In all their pretty array
I cried, because you couldn't see
Not a word, could you say.

I thought of the beautiful place
Where, I know you are today
We'll view the flowers together
When I have gone away.

So many people came by
Just, to say farewell
I didn't recognize some of them
Touched by your life, I could tell.

At two o'clock, June twenty-five
Kenneth gave your last request
Tell friends and loved ones
I have received my final rest.

Wanda, I came a little early
I wanted to see you alone
To tell you I love you
And can't believe you are gone.

Brenda and Kenneth sang your song
"I Firmly Promise You"
Couldn't help but think of Daddy
They sang it for him too.

When the time came
To pass by and view
Wanda, it was so hard
I couldn't even speak to you.

So, after you were placed
Beneath, the cold sod
I sat out by your side
And talked to you, and God.

Three large, stone crosses
Stood on the hill above you
While Randy and Daddy rested
Just beyond your view.

I became angry that day
You were there on the hill alone
I looked all around and wondered
Where have all your friends gone.

Then, I realized through tears
Jesus has your hand now
I will just get up and go home
Get on with my life somehow.

It won't be easy, Wanda
Family reunion won't be the same
I will miss your presence
Miss hearing, you call my name.

I can't promise not to cry
Each time I think of you
With each tear that falls
I Firmly Promise You, too.

June 28 to July 16, 1993

Stand Up For A Lady

I did not write this poem. It was written by my daughter, Trish. She stayed with my father-in-law, Arthur Swain Sr., while Woody and I went to West Virginia, for Wanda's funeral.

The following year, when my father-in-law died, she wrote this poem for me.

He would sit in the chair, day after day
When will Pat be home? he would say
She's gone out of town
But will be back soon.

What a wonderful lady, he would say
Do you think they'll be home today?
Yes, a true lady you were in our sight
For you were there for him, day and night.

No regrets you should have
What a caretaker you were
Not a worry he had
Not one in the world.

He adored you, and loved you
You meant everything to him
What was even more amazing
You took care of all of them.

The day you came home
Tears streamed down his face
As he struggled to stand
No way, YOU could ever be replaced.

As you walked through the door, he said
"Let me stand up for a lady"
A true lady, you were, not a maybe, or a might
You are a true lady in all of our sight.

Patricia Karen Lastinger, December 14, 1994.
A tribute to my Mother.
In memory of the true love
Pap had for you.

Modern Romance

My son, Duane had been married twice, and divorced twice. He was living with me and his step-father. We were having dinner at a restaurant in Thomasville, Georgia, along with our daughter, Charity.
The waitress told Charity, she thought Duane was cute. That was the first of the rest. The following days, and their future marriage, prompted this poem. The marriage lasted for one month.

Sometimes it happens, today is one of them
No poetry will come to my feeble mind
I don't know what I'm gonna do
If, some rhyming, I can't find.

For a poet, the play is on words
With them, you can say about anything
Wouldn't it be nice, if you had words
To replace the engagement ring?

You could simply tell the sweet babe
With stars dancing in her eyes
I love you with all my very soul
Without the ring, she'd think it was lies.

You wouldn't have to buy any roses
As on your knees, you try to propose
Brother, you don't have the kind of words
That takes the place of a dewy rose.

If you had all the nice flowery words
To express your love to your honey
You could save your time and energy
And stop spending your hard earned money.

There is nothing to beat the sight
Of a fellow who's fallen in love
He finds it harder to choose words
Than to reach the stars above.

And so he tries, and so you see
Him down on his knees
Showing his deepest love
As he offers his earnest pleas.

Darling, you know the only love
In all the world is you
If only you will be my wife
Forever to you, I'll be true

Both are willing to voice "I do"
With all their love and charm
Aren't they a nice couple
As they leave arm in arm?

March 1993

Tricia's Romance

When Tricia was barely sixteen, Buddy, came to our house, to see her. For about a month, they mostly stood in our yard, and just looked at each other. At least it seemed that way to me. I never heard, or saw them say a word. He got a little braver, and ventured inside the house.

My instructions were parlor dating only. Hold hands and no kissing. Might as well be talking to the wall. Every time I turned around they were kissing. I thought they would surely smother to death if they didn't come up for air. All of my threats didn't seem to stop the kissing.

After they were married, I decided to write about their romantic adventures. Read on for the rest of the story.

It was early July, nineteen eighty-four
When Buddy appeared in her life
Little did I realize at the time
Someday, she would be his wife.

I'd hardly call it love at first sight
From my point of view
They just sat and looked at each other
Didn't even know what to do.

I kept such a keen eye on them
Because she was my baby
If I had given him a chance
He would have kissed her, I think maybe.

She was a little sweet sixteen
Not old enough to date
She insisted it was not fair
For me to make her wait.

Every day he was at my house
I wondered, did he ever rest
I began to think they were too serious
If I just told him to get, would be best.

I tried in a polite way to tell her
You have him over here too much
She cried and pleaded her case
So I told him to sit, but don't touch.

Don't touch, take my word for it
They were constantly holding hands and kissing
If he was a little late getting there
You would have thought he was missing.

This routine went on and on
Mixed with a lot of fuss and fight
They seemed to be getting the practice
So they could start their marriage right.

Talk about marriage, well let me tell you
The nerve of that girl and boy
They were going to just plain elope
And take away all my joy.

Well, I figured, I had put up with them
For a good two and a half years
When they decided to say their "I dos"
I should be able, to at least hear.

She told Teresa to tell me
What they had planned to do
While out the door, she ran
Afraid, her love bundles I would sue.

Go ahead, make the wedding plans
I figured might be just as well
At least the fighting would be in their house
And no one be there to tell.

On December fifth, nineteen eighty-six
Buddy decided to say "I do"
Even though Tricia was scared to death
I think she was heard to say "Me too".

Every other day has been a fight
Every other day, just kiss, and kiss
If you have never had a lover's fight
Maybe you don't know what you miss.

The honeymoon, I guess is over
Two years have come and gone
Dating is a thing of the past
But marriage goes on and on.

Have to wash his dirty clothes
And make him look real nice
If he glances at another girl
She reminds him, I'm your spice.

After all is said and done
Nowhere will you ever find
Such sweet spice, and love bundles
They are really two of a kind.

January 5 to January 6, 1989

Dear Wanda

On the first anniversary of Wanda's death, I wrote a poem to her. The dead may not be able to hear us, nor we hear them, but we can talk to them all we want to. When we are talking, all of the deep feelings can come forth and free us from a lot of hurt. I learned a lot from her death. I learned to say what I want to say while a person is alive. Take the time to talk. Don't be afraid to show love and concern. Once they are dead, all chances are gone.

> You've been gone a year, now
> Sometimes, it seems like forever
> I know if I ask you to come back,
> You would just tell me "Never."
>
> You know, I wouldn't ask you
> To leave a world of perfect bliss
> To take on your earthly form and
> Come back to a world like this.
>
> Wanda, I miss you most, when
> It is time to write the newsletter
> Even though you can't send the birthdays
> I think, I am doing a little better.

I know you don't live out on that hillside
Where those three crosses stand
But there we placed a monument for you
We've done all, that we really can.

Yet, this seems so small to me.
When I think of all the cards from you
I miss them so very much now
As the mailbox has only a few.

Wanda, I don't even know what to say
Nor how to express the way I feel
Your not being here with us now
It doesn't seem quite real.

This aching, longing, hurting inside
As down my cheeks the tears spill
Wanda, you couldn't quite realize
Death handed me a terrible deal.

Fresh in my mind, the hours I waited
For you to look, and speak to me
My heart will never be able to mend
Until the day, I also am free.

My time here is also short
As I await the soon coming King
Then, Wanda, in our new home
Together, we can talk and sing.

June 21, 1994

My Daddy

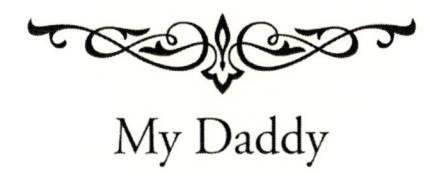

When Daddy had been dead for about four years, I wrote a poem for him. I forgot to put the date on it, and not certain of when it was written.

>As we celebrate Father's Day, this year
>I will do a little day-dreaming
>Thinking of times, as a child
>I spent with all my ways of scheming.
>
>Thought I could out-smart my dad
>Mom, I knew, was always quite wise
>I figured she must have been just like me
>When she was about my size.
>
>I once made cornbread for supper
>I wanted it to be a real treat
>The only complaint Daddy had
>Chocolate cornbread he would not eat
>
>Years came and years went
>Soon, I was nearly grown
>I knew Daddy must look forward
>To the day when I would be gone.

I did grow up and
One day, I went away
Daddy didn't seem too happy
But what could he say?

One day, I came home
Many years had passed
I looked at my Daddy
But he was home at last.

I could only touch him
And stroke his cold brow
Happy Father's Day, Daddy.
That is all for now.

Date unknown

Family Reunion

You would just have to be there for yourself, if you want to know about our family reunion. We had such great times when the family came from far and near. We talked, laughed, and cried. Some of us gathered around the table and sang until the wee hours of the next morning.

Some had to leave early, while others stayed a day or two. But, all of us really have a great time. After Mom died, it has never been the same. It is like putting a puzzle together, and as you finish, you find one piece missing. Try as you may, you cannot find that one piece. The picture is incomplete.

Listen, my child, and you shall hear
Of a family reunion, held year after year
Third Saturday of August, they all gather in
All hollering, "Howdy" and "How have you been?"
More commotion than the law allow
But we get through it all somehow
The time of year, we see most of our kin
Now and then, a few stragglers drop in.
Mom in the kitchen, for two days and a night
Just making sure our dinner is alright
If you like cake, a little pudding too
The best around, we will feed you.
We fix chicken, salads, potatoes and beans
Someday, I'll sneak in some collard greens

Children, and grandchildren, and great-grand galore
Every year, we seem to get more, and more.
We have in-laws, and out-laws, sometimes no law.
These are the fastest eaters you ever saw
We have a lot of hugging and kissing cousins
That is how we know, all the heathens are in.
We do more, than just cook and eat
After the meal, we are in for a treat
Barbara, in that bag, brings a lot of stuff
When your number wasn't drawn, it's really rough.
Rough, if you wanted to win that prize
That wasn't your number, no use to tell lies
After our program is over and done
We will then honor a special someone.
Then, a few will have to go
What is the rush, nobody knows
What of us, that are able
Will all by now head for the table.
Sweets you eat until you can't walk
But it does little to hinder the talk
When it grows dark, some head for the grass
Where they tell ghost stories about the past.
The rest of us will gather to sing
Lifting our voices until the rafters ring
Somewhere, around three, we fall in bed
Next morning, when awakened, we act most dead.
But we drag the old body right to the table
Eating again, don't you think we are able?

Florida crowd will start on their way
Most of the others will spend the day.
It seems a little sad, I must tell you
As we realize again, Family Reunion is through
We say good-bye to the silent ones on the hill
And meet them in Heaven, we promise, we will.
But, until next year, to those who are alive
It will all start again, as we begin to arrive.

July 28, 1996

Please Don't Unravel My Brain

This really happened one day. Bobby Lee came in the house when I was sewing. He wanted four hundred dollars for some reason. After a bunch of words were exchanged, he decided I was loaning him the money. In about fifteen minutes, I had my poem. When your brain is unraveled what can you expect?

Sometimes in this world, of children
I wonder if I will really survive
When I watch their scheming ways
I feel fortunate, to just be alive.

How many forties are in a hundred?
Was the question Bobby put to me
After helping him figure out the sum
Four hundred dollars was his need and plea.

He hugged me and said "You're a nice Mom"
Thanking me for borrowing four hundred dollars
I looked at Woody, he only shook his head
This con artist bit was more than I could swallow.

I quickly went out the front door
To set up a big stork trap
Marching straightway to my sewing machine
To make for Bobby, a great big wrap.

When you look up and see a stork
If he seems to be carrying a heavy load
It will be Bobby riding alone
Bound up in that stork wrap, I sewed.

If you need a wrap, catch the stork
If you need a child catch a train
Ride, as far as the rails will go
But, please don't unravel my brain.

August 29, 1992

Our Christmas Together

 Christmas of 1988 was only a few days after we buried my Daddy. I fixed Christmas dinner for all the children. Woody's dad and his brother Bill were there. That was the first and last time Bill was with us for Christmas. He had blood clots in his legs and was in the hospital for a few days before he returned to his home in Hollywood, Florida.
 Two days after he flew back, he died in his sleep on January 13, 1989. The day before his Daddy's 88th birthday.

When I think of Bill
How he left us so fast
I could not help, but remember
Our Christmas just past.

Bill flew up from Hollywood
To spend this holiday season
His first since I came to the family
Perhaps, this was for a reason.

Christmas dinner was prepared
Relatives were all gathered in
We all ganged around the table
The great feast to begin.

Bill loved the ham and cakes
Of how good the ham, he boast
Of all the Christmases in the south
This one I will remember most.

Dad, Lola, and Bill were there
Teresa, Danny and children too
Duane, Jeffery, Tricia and Buddy
I wouldn't forget any of you.

Of course, Woody, Charity and Bobby Lee
Piled the food on their dinner plate
Even though it was mostly my cooking
Neither could I hardly wait.

We exchanged our gifts
All seemed to go so well
The children were so quiet
I thought they were under a spell.

Christmas came and went
So did the year of 1988
With Bill in the hospital
His going home would be late.

Blood clots, the doctor said
Better watch what you do
Take life very easy
We don't want to lose you.

Dad and I took him to the airport
We then said our last goodbye
We had to go on our way
And shortly let him fly.

He made it home safely
So, he told Dad by phone
Only a couple days, and then
The call said he was gone.

We made the trip to Hollywood
To bid him a farewell
To much to really realize
No need for me to tell.

We had you cremated
As that was your desire
We buried the urn at Sunset Gardens
From us, you won't be far.

We want to remember you
Just the way you were
So each day while we live
In our hearts, you will be dear.

January 20, 1989

*In memory of William Edward Swain
(May 15, 1925 to January 13, 1989*

A Note To Woody

We had been married just over three years when I wrote this to Woody. I didn't know him as well then as now, but I made him think I could read his mind. Now, he knows, I really can.

I would write you a poem
If I were a mind to
But, as I have no mind
This little note will do.

Now that you know I love you
Because I have just said it
Maybe, now you will linger
And not try to split it.

Curl up under the tree, babe
Keep your eyes upon the door
Just when you start to take a peek
I'll appear, that's for sure.

I can read your mind
Just like a book
One glance at your eyes
Is all that it took.

December 4, 1979

Through The Garden Gate

Earl Herb died on October 16, 1992. He was a friend of Teresa's, but all of us girls had lunch with him ever so often. We were to have lunch with him the day we learned of his death. I wrote the following poem in fond memory of him.

> The loss of a friend is spoken, although these words are not true
> Not even the mocking hand of death can take a friend from you
> Jesus is our best friend, although our natural eye can't see
> He is right there at our side, whatever the heartache may be.

> Earl did not die as we're told. He went through the Garden Gate
> Where, in the presence of our Lord, patiently caring, he'll wait
> I know, Earl was a true friend. He showed you in every way
> Always making the road easier where you walked, day by day.

> When God sends a friend, He chooses the very best
> That's what he was to you, until he went away to rest
> We are not, as those without hope. We know, soon, we will also be
> In that place of eternal rest, where from tears, we'll be free.

> He tried to tell you his days were getting short
> Teresa, you cast it aside, didn't want to hear the sort
> You knew his heart was failing. He was in a lot of pain
> He was trying to tell you, as he cried, again, and again.

Teresa, no need for regret, wishing you had done differently
What else could you have done, when all went, as was to be?
Because of you, he knew the way that leads to the Father's throne
When Earl asked for God's grace, He took him for His own.

We all know what true friendship is. Death does not bring it's end
We only join him there, and forever be a friend
The Garden Gate will close behind us, on that day
There, in the Garden, friends will always stay.

October 20, 1992

Please Send Jesus

The following poem was written on June 6, 1999, sometime between 4:00 am and 7:00 am, after I had gotten a phone call that Mama's pulse rate was between 112 and 156, all night. If I can't sleep, I can usually write. This was one of those times.

Oh God, I know when it come my Mama time to leave
Deep in my heart, I will cry and grieve
But, if I know, you will send Jesus to take her there
I will be able to cope with things here.

Jesus has been on this earth before
He knows the way to go through death's door
He has crossed that old chilly river
That causes us to imagine and quiver.

Mama knows Jesus in her words and heart
He should be the one to help as she depart
An angel wouldn't understand her love
How hard it is to leave her children, and go above.

You see, Father, some don't even know Him
Some may have allowed their light to dim
Mama knows, and she is waiting to hear
All her children say, I will meet you there.

June 6, 1999

Have A Party

I wrote the following poem sometime within the last two years that Mom lived. I had been talking with her on the phone. She lived alone and she was lonesome that day. She must have had me convinced, because I ended up later writing this poem for one of my Newsletters. Never did ask her if she recognized herself, when she read it in the Newsletter.

The leaves fell like tear drops
On one cold, and frosty morn
A little old lady sat, weary
Brow beaten and forlorn.

Self Pity had just walked in
To be her guest for the day
And, Gloom was starting to leave
When, suddenly, decided to stay.

I'll just pull the phone
Right off of the wall
No use to have one
If no one ever call.

Can't even enjoy my food
With no one to talk to
With Misery just waking up
I know what I will do.

I'll give myself a party
I'll plan it around noon
Self Pity, Gloom and Misery
All three left real soon.

The little old lady was so busy
She didn't know they had gone
When the party was ready
She found herself alone.

She thought she was alone
Until she glanced around
Seeing the one she had lost
Happiness at last was found.

"Who is that with you?"
She asked with a grin
They are Peace and Joy
They decided to drop in.

So long since I have seen you
I hope that you will stay
No problem, if you will promise
To read God's word and pray.

Sounds like a deal, she said
As she drank her cup of tea
Since I see Hope is also here
I'm so thankful to thee.

The party was not soon over
Than Joy flooded her soul
Peace settled into her heart
Happiness moved in, I'm told.

Exact Date Unknown

Daniel

This one, I wrote for Daniel when he graduated from Jefferson County High School in Monticello Florida, in May, of 1999. It was written on May 4, 1999, at the request of his mother, Teresa Burk. Since I know how she feels about Daniel, I could easily write this poem.

Today, you are going to graduate
Daniel, how proud I am of you
Knowing you have pushed ahead
To make your dreams come true.

So tall, so handsome, my son
Not in all my wildest dreams
Could I have a child like you
To make my heart full of beams.

You clung to me as a baby
Never wanted me from your sight
Now, I am the one who does the clinging
Holding to you with all my might.

You captured my whole heart
As I held you in my arms
In a world full of danger
I tried to protect you from harms.

Many times when I was sad
You could always bring my smile
Being a person, few have known
Clowning around all the while.

You have never shown a bad attitude
No matter what came your way
You took everything in stride
Looking toward a future day.

We gave you to God as a baby
And placed you in His care
Surely He will use your gentle ways
To work for Him, if you only dare.

You'll always be my main man
As I turn you to the world
But, I am praying for a helper
As God chooses that special girl.

May 4, 1999

Will T. Bear

I was at work the other day when I wrapped a birthday gift for Kenneth. I wrote him a poem as I named his bear. I got him one of those teddy bears with 2000 on it. I didn't know he doesn't like teddy bears. I really wanted it for myself, but it was his birthday.

Ho, ho, ho, and hey, hey, hey
What do you want for your birthday?
I'm sure you could think of lots of things
But, not more happiness than a teddy bear brings.

He is cuddly, warm and nice
Lasts a lot longer than Ole Spice
Much better than an empty billfold
Much nicer than a piece of gold.

This teddy bear is well named
He is also very, very famed
Will T. Bear, the name he knows
Like a true friend, where you go, he goes.

I call him Will T. because of his abilities
Him, you do not always have to please
He can give you will to bare
He can give you the courage to care.

He will love you when you are old
He will love you when you are told
Some of life's many sorrows
You have him today, he'll be there tomorrow

He doesn't make a lot of noise
Mostly, he just sits quiet and poised
He sure is warm, when you are alone
He is still around, when the grandkids are gone.

He could never replace your best friend
The one who is there to the end
But, when you just need a smile
Just hold old Will T. for awhile.

He will not tell all your troubles
He will not burst all our bubbles
He will just patiently, sit and wait
For cuddling, no matter your state.

Smile and kiss ole Will T.
He is your birthday gift from me
When you see him, sit and stare
You will know, I wish I could be there.

December 7, 2000

Erica

I didn't know Erica. She was the daughter of a lady whom Teresa worked for. Erica, not quite sixteen, had cancer. Teresa was so touched by her condition that she involved my emotions. Every week, she gave me an update. She let me know, as time seemed over for Erica. Thus, the day she died, I knew I had to write a poem in her memory.

> Your sixteenth birthday, you wanted to make
> As you realized, soon your soul, God would take
> To that home far beyond this heart-aching world
> Where all the beauties of heaven, God unfurls.
>
> You lived life, gripping to its fullness
> Knowing full well time is borrowed, and thus
> With all determination, you reached toward a goal
> To show friends how to live, advancing death bold.
>
> Erica, you will be remembered through years
> Embraced with love through all our tears
> You were a daughter, a sister, a friend
> You showed us your love until the end.
>
> The end of life on earth as we know it
> Though short, you cherished each bit
> Reaching out to all, with such great love
> As death came, softly, to carry you home above.

Your home will be empty, the space no one can fill
We can accept this, knowing it is God's will
In that eternal home, we too, some day shall enter
No vacant spaces, no tears will be known there.

April 28, 1996
for the family of Erica who departed on April 23, 1996

Only God

Every death touches me. I may not know the person, but I feel the family's pain just the same. I worked for a lady when her mother got killed in a car wreck in Atlanta. I had met her mother and saw the closeness of the two. On the first day I saw Sharon, afterward, I saw grief in person.

Only God understands a mother's love
Only God understands a child's grief
When heartaches stop at our door
Only God can give that precious relief.

Flowers, they bloom, but for a season
Soon their beauty fades away
But, in God's eternal plans
They will revive another day.

God placed your mother in your life
Truly, for you, she was one of a kind
Then came the day, in His plans
HE placed her in the Great Divine.

Take courage, not in this present turmoil
But in the comfort that He gives
You can go to where she is
In God's house is where she now lives.

April 14, 1996
for Sharon, whose mother died on March 22, 1996

It's Ok To Ask Why

The next poem was written for Rev. John Anderson and his daughter, Rochelle, when his wife, Melinda, was killed in a car accident. I did not know then, but I wrote this only two and a half weeks before my Daddy died.

She was God's child
Of this I am sure
The daily path she trod
Her cross to endure.

She was the wife
God chose for you
To walk by your side
Helping, God's work to do.

Human as we are
We often say, why?
Why did you call, Lord?
Why did she die?

We abide in this world
The throne room, we don't see
Where God plans our life
Maps how He wants it to be.

To mold us and make us
Into His perfect will
He tears apart our plans
Pain is all we feel.

God allowed you love and joy
As you walked, day by day
In all of God's wisdom
He marked your way.

There is a river
We must all pass through
He was there for Melinda
He'll be there, for you.

When we see the light
We hear Jesus call
We just walk toward home
Leaving cares and all.

When Jesus reaches His hand
We cross over that river
We forget to look back
Knowing we are home, forever.

They say God wipes away
All the tears from our eyes
Maybe, not in this life
But at home in the sky.

Brother John, I know you ask why
God doesn't mind, He understands
He'll lend you, His shoulder
As He holds to your hands.

What else could I say?
I am a human too
If God puts me in your shoes
I could only do as you.

We try to prepare ourselves
For time, when death arrives
No way are we ready
Should we prepare all our lives.

John and Rochelle, I remind you
As lonely days are ahead
One day, you will see the light
Across the river, you'll be lead.

November 14, 1988

Hi Daddy

This following poem was written on the first anniversary of my Daddy's death. A year had passed, but not the grief, of death.

Daddy, it's been a year today
Since you up and went away
You didn't take time to tell me bye
Didn't you know that would make me cry?

Guess sometimes, we get in a hurry
No need, you'd say, to worry.
Can't change the way things are
I didn't really go so far.

Time waits for no one, dear
When death bids, you are leaving here
No time to linger, just to chat
I think you really know that, Pat.

What is it you always say?
Take time out from work to play
Rest your weary bones while here
Time waits for no one, dear.

Make the road easier for others
Help your sisters and your brothers
You may be in need tomorrow
Your path may even cross with sorrow.

What you sow, you will reap
Sow it good, and reap a heap
Sow it bad, and I can tell
Reap a heap, you will, as well.

Treasures you lay up here
Will mean nothing later, dear
When death walks to your door
Whispering, 'Come on, time is no more.'

Can't take it with you
No matter what you do
You'll leave all your wealth behind
For friends and foes to find.

Treasures laid up in heaven
Will grow as bread with leaven
Bread, you eat, and it is gone
Treasures in heaven, last on and on.

Live today, as though your last
Time, you know, will swiftly pass
One day soon, you too will hear
I was sent for you, my dear'.

Neither will you have time for bye
You'll be gone, just as I
You won't have to wonder then
Just where your ole Daddy's been.

I didn't get to tell you bye
I'll be the first to tell you, "Hi"
Here, where time and eternity meet
And death will forever know defeat.

December 2, 1989

SECTION TWO

    Section Two is made up of twenty-two poems. I love to tease people as they get older, and start worrying about getting wrinkles, fat, and gray hairs. I always think of myself as being young, and never worry about getting old.

    The older I get, the longer it seems to take to get old. I know one day I will wake up and realize, it caught up with me. When it does, I'll throw in the towel and won't be worth a dime. I will check myself into a nursing home, so I don't worry the life out of my children. When I can't drive and go where I want to go, when I can't see well enough to work on the computer, and can't hear enough to talk on the phone, that is when I will know, that I finally got old.

    You talk about a pest, I will be one. The reason I am checking myself into a nursing home, I want to choose the place, where I live the rest of my life, before the children have a chance to do so. They have no idea what it will be like, when they try to take my car keys, and confine me to one section of the house, because I slop and spill all the time. They haven't seen anything yet!

How About It, Kids?

The next poem is for my children, and about all children. After reading it, you will know why I have to go to a nursing home when I get old.

I don't have time to write a poem
I am too hoarse to sing a song
I am too tired to do any work
Don't ask me what can be wrong.

Everything is wrong, you see
We have daylight saving time
Doesn't save me anything
Not any work, not even a dime.

The whole world has gone wrong
Maybe, it is just turned around
All the kids should have to work
But, work, kids are nowhere found.

Moms should be the beauty stars
Children could be butlers and maids
A world of more disaster, you'd find
Even if all the kids were paid.

What if the men did all the work?
What if the women just boss?
What if they got orders from the kids?
The world would be a total loss!

Sorry kids, you do not give orders
Neither, will you ever be paid
For all the back breaking work
You performed as butlers and maids.

What you will receive at home
Is a fortune of love and care
Worth more than all the gold
Deny this, no one would dare.

When you think you have no care
When you think you have no love
Walk in the footsteps of your parents
Listen to them talk to God above.

While you are sound asleep
Or maybe you're pacing the floor
Rest in the love of Mom and Dad
Love and care, you couldn't ask for more.

Without asking, you have it thought
Wrapped in God's security
How could you feel, but loved
Throughout all of eternity?

October 3, 1993

What If?

At one time, I attended the Boston, Georgia, Green Street Church of God. Every year, we had Pastor's Appreciation Day. This is a time when we do something special for our pastor. I can't do much, but just ask me to do something, and I will write a poem. I will even stand up and read it. How you read it is how others perceive it.

What if there were no Boston?
And if there were no Green Street?
And there were no Church of God
Where, with our great God, we meet.

What if there were no people
To sit on a yellow seat?
What if we had no drummer boy
That never skips a single beat?

What if we had no piano?
What if we had no Elaine?
The one we all appreciate
Would probably go insane.

What if we had no little babies?
What if no one kept the nursery?
Would be more howling in the church
Than what you hear from the baby.

What if we didn't have our teens?
We'd shed a lot of bitter tears
But with the help and mercy of God
We can handle our little dears.

What if we had no teachers?
What if we had no class?
We would be in such bad shape
We'd hope this came to pass.

What if we had no youth leaders?
Lord knows, they have a task
If you don't believe what I say
All you have to do, is ask.

What if we had no God?
What if the Bible were not here?
If we had no faith to pray
Our lives would be made of doubts and fear.

What if we had all of the above
But a pastor we could not find?
We'd have a great big vacant spot
For, we have the only one of a kind.

There is God, a Bible, and Boston too
There is a Church of God on Green
There are babies and nursery workers.
Thank God, yes, we have our teens.

We have our choir and choir leader
For teachers, we have some of the best
We have our singers and our greeters
Now perk up and hear the rest.

We have the best pastor, God could find
To be a leader of this church
When a job needed to be done
He was never one to lurch.

A good pastor looks out for the flock
He cares about each of their needs
Week after week, from the pulpit
He constantly spreads the seeds.

He carefully strives to help each one
To accomplish their eternal goals
He does not see us as just a people
He looks beyond to reach our souls.

April 6, 1995

Ode Of A Lost Birthday Card

The next poem was written for my pastor Rev. Ray Hunt. I bought a card to mail. As is my eternal habit, I lost the card. I was determined to send a card, so I purchased another one. Along with the card, I had to write a poem. This way, he would know that he is special!

Brother Ray had a birthday
Made him around fifty-five
Not much use to complain
At least, you are still alive.

I got a card for the occasion
Was going to put it in the mail
Couldn't find it for the life of me
Then I thought, Oh well.

Just buy another birthday card
Like the one you had before
Couldn't remember a word it said
My nerves could take no more.

I knew it was a smarty type
Making fun of old age, I guess
Trying to remember where I put it
You know, I tried my level best.

It was then, the thought struck me
When do we start getting old?
When we start losing things, or
Forget everything we are told.

Forgetting that's in the very young
I'll declare to my dying day
I never had a child
To remember anything I say.

Really, let me clarify
I mean, they cannot hear
If loss of hearing is getting old
I really began to fear.

Were all my children born old?
They couldn't remember, think or see
Couldn't hear, walk or smell
Seemed really frightening to me.

Must be some way to know
When we start to get old
I really don't think it's when
You claim you are always cold.

I thought back to my children again
How are they different than I?
Give me a little space now
And figure this, I'll try.

They can only run to the table
They drag themselves to the bed
In the morning, when you call them
It appears they are all dead.

They can't see any dirty dishes
Should they reach to the ceiling?
One mention of cleaning rooms
Brings on a lot of fast dealing.

Now, after a lot of writing
A considerable amount of thought
I figure it is my solemn duty
To tell you, I know I ought.

They say you are born dying
I say, you never really get old
We are just imitating our kids
Never mind what you are told.

March 13, 1991
For Rev. Ray Hunt's birthday

Zip It, If You Must

I have seen a lot of people get into a bad position for running their mouth. I have even been in a difficult place for my words also. I am not sure what, if anything in particular, happened that caused me to pen these words. More than likely, someone said something that I didn't like. This was my way of just telling them to be quiet and not talk so much.

Sometimes, when I sit to write a poem
It seems my head is sort of blank
Doesn't seem to be much to write
Resembles my account at the bank.

Most of you know by now anyway
I will scribble a few crazy words
Might be about something you know well
Could be something you have never heard.

Don't be guessing, just keep reading.
You and I both shall later see
What I can spin around the old brain
And pull the best right out of me.

Best, worst, whatever you think
Think is usually my hind sight
After I have written it, or spit it
Then try to recall, with all my might.

That is the reason, to put the brain in motion
Before we put the fat lips in gear
When you practice this method more
You won't repeat most of what you hear.

If something sounds real juicy
You can't wait, someone to tell
Would you go ahead and repeat it
If it fit you just as well?

There is no one who is all perfect
No one who is made of all bad
It is just when gossip is repeated
Someone aches and feels so sad.

I have been guilty, I'm sure you have too
Of trying to recall that last spill
If we are to live without all regrets
Zip the lips and keep them still.

Aren't I good at giving advice?
Best be good at keeping my thought
If it would harm the spirit of another
And create with my loved one, an ought.

What I am really trying to say
Maybe, I don't quite know how
Speak only good, of sisters and brothers
Even if we must all begin right now.

June 23, 1992

Who Do We Appreciate?

I had been going to The Church of God, at Boston, for nearly six years, when we had another Pastor's Appreciation Day. I just had to get my two cents worth in. So, for what it is worth, here is what I had to say.

> I could start by saying, once upon a time
> In a little Dixie town called Boston
> God looked down, for a Church of God
> Seeing none, He decided to make one.
>
> It wasn't to be just any kind of church
> He wanted one that was strong and sure
> He wanted it to be a Lighthouse
> Purchased by His blood, it would endure.
>
> God does nothing without a plan
> If you look, you can very well see
> God didn't choose just any kind of man
> To shepherd a sheep like you and me.
>
> What will I do, I suppose God thought
> First, I will look in Coolidge for a man
> I have one in mind, I will send
> To fill the post at Boston. I know he can.

He doesn't claim to know a lot
Well, that's just the kind I need
To shepherd the sheep I'll send to him
A lot he will learn indeed.

I'll let him start out slow at first
Only send him children to lead
When he has mastered the little ones
Then, a little tougher flock to feed.

So through the years, they came
And through the years, some have tried
To see what our shepherd was made of
Soon they realized, God is on his side.

Many have come and many have gone
For whatever the reason may be
God just picked the toughest of the flock
And left them at Boston, as you see.

Through the years, we've stood the test
We've learned to love and share
Where the angels fear to tread
Some of us will even dare!

We have heard a lot of sermons
Like the one entitled, "It Came To Pass"
Or maybe like, "Wake Up Ralph"
Those made you perk your ears up fast.

"Until I Went Into The Sanctuary"
Was the one I valued the best
Taken from the 73rd Psalm
This sermon could stand any test.

Week after week, and year after year
He has given to us God's word
When at last, we stand before God
We cannot say we have not heard.

Life would be so easy each day
Very little, Brother Hunt, you'd have to do
If it wasn't for this crazy bunch of sheep
The Good Lord has sent to you.

There have been little, tiny problems
Any person could easily solve
Then for the big, big, biggies
All of heaven had to get involved.

We love and respect our shepherd
Although sometimes, he just cries
When we just go along our own way
Seeming to care less if he just dies.

Now, really, we are just like most kids
Who knows their parents are getting old
They just don't say or do very much
Unless they are very sternly told.

I mean told of how thoughtless we are
And how we need to show our care
Instead of thinking all is well
And the Shepherd will always be here.

God must have looked at us, a lot of times
Wondering how we all got shipped in
If in His plans, there was a place for us
When first, this church did begin.

Well, yes, there it is alright
Each sheep, just as He designed
All, right where He has placed them
Each, in his own pew, you will find.

Nothing is impossible with God
Nor with this church at Boston
When we are given a job to do
You may as well count it as done.

We don't sell hot dogs or donuts
Neither do we sell chicken plates
When we need a building made
To be sure we don't just sit and wait.

Guess I've done a lot of bragging
On your bunch of sheep, Brother Ray
To tell you all about each of us
Don't guess it would really pay.

What could I say that you don't know?
God has taught you a lot, I think
When it comes to a good pastor
Right at the top, is where you rank.

Now, I have taken up a bit of time
Even though I see it's growing late
What I am really trying to say
Brother Ray, it's you, we all appreciate.

No, I didn't forget you, Sister Betty
We couldn't do without you here
So, that is why I really believe
God chooses a good woman, my dear.

Appreciate you, better believe we do
We know you keep Brother Ray in line
Your job has been complicated
But, you are doing just fine.

March 6-7, 1985

Class Of '58

    I graduated from Matoaka High School in May of 1958. I am not really certain how the students in charge of the year book knew that I could write poetry. I must have said something about it to someone. I just know, I was asked to write a poem for the year book. I was delighted and penned the following lines, and gave them to be published.

    In August of 1993, we had our thirty-fifth year class reunion, and I was asked to read the poem at a dinner we had together to celebrate.

We are the senior class of '58
Just waiting for the day we graduate
But, while we linger here, although
There are a few things we want you to know.
Some things you should have already known
If you're not like us, real gone
We love our teachers, so very dear
The ones who have tried year after year
To teach us the knowledge of books
And keep us from becoming crooks
But, what an awful shame it would be
If our little knowledge, they could see!
Our principal is a kindly soul
Although we admit, he is quite bold
To trust in us the way he does
You would even say we was

The most honest students at M.H. S.
If you only gave a little guess
To all the world we have a word
We doubt if you have heard.
That very soon, we will be
Starting upon a long journey
To explore the world, so wide
And learn, just what it has inside.
We'll see what makes the world go around
And why it doesn't sometimes fall down
We want to know what's on the moon
We might even move there soon.
Live up there, with a family of our own
And think of happy times in M.H.S. we've known
The time when we were seniors at M.H.S.
And when we tried to do our very best
To have nice manners and learn real well
We tried so hard not to fail
Because we wanted to show that we
Were as good as angels ever could be.
Through all these twelve years, we've worked so hard
Taking exams and growing so tired
But, on that blessed day in May
We hope to receive our twelve years pay.
When a diploma is given to each one
We'll all agree that school has been real fun.

Patricia Abram. Around March, 1958

Project Turnaround

When I was 45 years of age, in 1985, with only a high school education and without a job, decisions had to be made. We had opened a little restaurant in Boston, Georgia, named the Apple House. We had $400 cash to work with. I knew nothing of the expense of a business. Needless to say, we lasted three months. Having worked at least 16 hours a day, six days a week, took me about under. All the gain we received from that business was three meals a day.

We closed the restaurant, and I got a job making drill bits. That lasted one month before the factory went out of business. Jobless, moneyless and desperate, I went looking for another job.

Someone told me about a job working in an office of a car dealership. I was interviewed for the job. I didn't know how to operate a computer, and the lady told me I was "too old to learn." I decided that day that I will learn computers or die. At the Georgia Employment Office, I learned that I could go to a government-funded school, called Project Turnaround. We learned how to do a lot of things to help get a job. I had a goal. When I learned that I could go to Thomas Technical Institute and learn computers, my mind was set. The last thing I did at Project Turnaround was write the following poem, which they had published in the Thomasville Times.

At Thomas Tech, I learned Accounting and Data Processing. I even learned how to program the computer. I became one of the GOAL nominees. Although, I didn't win the GOAL award, I was one of the runners-up. I made my own goal – "Never tell a woman that she is too old to do anything she really wants to do."

If you have been looking
But a job you can't find
Maybe, it's your appearance
Or, maybe, just your mind.

You'll learn to press the wrinkles
Turn the ole collar down
Even how to sit up straight
Here at Project Turnaround.

Maeno comes on with all the rules
All those don't and do's
Roan will teach you to listen
With ears wide open, you can't lose.

Gurley puts us through role play
To see just how funny we sound
Sure is fun learning to be actors
Here, at Project Turnaround.

Now, it ain't all laughter
And it ain't all play
We are really most serious
Majority of the day.

Kay gives a lot of good tips
To help us look real super
Hattie comes on with group time
Well, she is just duper.

If you want a job, sit up
Even look like you're awake
Should you feel your eyes go shut
Turn your head, for Hattie's sake.

We don't worry about races
We don't worry about our age
Only here at Turnaround
We leave our own page.

Just five short weeks
Then it is all over
Unless, by some great luck
A real job, we discover.

Whether it be luck or be it charm
By which a job you found.
Bare this one thought in mind
A lot you owe, PROJECT TURNAROUND.

Let's not forget the others
Who work behind the scene
Dr. Ellis and her staff
Upon whom she must lean.

To check the aptitudes
Never once do they complain
With all of us they see come by
I am sure they feel some pain.

February, 1985

Quiet Night

As you probably know by now, I do a family Newsletter each month and mail a copy to each family household. On this particular night, I was trying to get a poem written to put on back page, as is my usual thing. Charity was at work and called to let me know she was on the way home. She broke the silence in the room, and thus a poem was written.

'Twas the night before Sunday,
and all through the room
Silence was so golden, I felt a little bit of gloom
The children were off somewhere in relative's beds
With visions of vacation running in their heads.
Woody was worn out from counting the black sheep
Soon a couple of Nytol put him sound asleep.
I was at the computer, a newsletter trying to write
When the crazy, old phone, broke the peaceful quiet.
Oh, yes, you surely must know, had to be Charity
The little angel the stork brought to Woody and me
I was supposed to teach her some human manners
While she had a job to drive me bananas.
The air conditioner was noisily a humming
And somewhere a cricket, a guitar was strumming
I know I heard something up there on the roof
But, I really can't say I have any proof.
July, I once heard of Christmas in July
Could that be the reason? Oh, my!

What if Christmas is in July this year
And that is the sound of a red faced reindeer?
I don't even believe in old Santa Claus
Listen, and I can just tell you the cause
I was told if I wasn't real good
And behave like all nice children should.
Santa would be watching and he would see
And, that would end all the toys for me
I was a real good child, when I was asleep
I'd find the toys and always I'd peep.
Now that I am sitting here in the night
Straining my brain and trying to write
I know now what it was I thought I heard
It's even worse than I at first had feared.
My fingers were pounding the computer keys
So hard, it shook the joints of my knees
After all, I am glad as I guess you see
It wasn't really Rudolph after me.
I think I will just stop this mess
And put myself to bed with the rest.

July 18, 1992
The Bible says it is not good that man be alone.
What about women being alone. Dangerous sometimes!

What A Pastor Is Like

It was the spring of 1985, when we had another Pastor's Appreciation Day. I knew a poem had to be written. I was painting some room at my home and trying to do two things at a time. I write while I am working, driving, and sometimes eating. I'll have to say when I am in church, my mind is on God and what is going on, and I do not write in my mind at church. I do get ideas that I later use.

Up on the ladder, just a' slinging paint
Needing to write a poem, thinking, I can't.
Pastor Appreciation Day, well it's here again
Want to express my feelings, but where to begin.
When you write a poem, it must come from the heart
I didn't know what to say, or just where to start.
I prayed, Lord, show me, what it really means
To be the true Pastor on whom the church leans.
Then, clear as can be, so I could realize
What a Pastor's job is, He opened my eyes.
It's sort of like this you see. He's much like a mother
With all of the duties replaced by no other.
Now, this I thought, must be quite a job
The position couldn't be filled by just any old slob.
I know the job of a mother, the heartaches and care
The house falls apart, when she is not there.
Her children are her worries.
Of course, the grandchildren too

To keep each one straight, more than she can do
When there is a fight, she is referee
Listening to each side you see.
The right punishment must be handed out
If it doesn't seem equal, some child will pout
There are daily steps, as each child grows
To lead him in righteousness,
all of heaven surely knows.
She shares their burdens; she wipes away the tears
Cares throughout their sickness,
comforts in all their fears
Since a pastor is like a mother, why is it hard for us
To just be like a child, and give him our trust?
Maybe, now that we know, the load on his shoulder
We'll be a little more patient, not sit like a boulder
We can show our respect,
instead of just saying we care
We can help make his job less of a nightmare
I could write more, if only the time I had
But, I'll say one thing, this child will stop being bad.

March 22, 1985

Just In Case You Didn't Know

My pastor had another birthday and a poem I shall write. Those children who think they will always be young, I love to hound them. I watch them do the same thing I did when they were little. They swear they will never spoil their child the way I did mine. Guess what? Like mother, like daughter (or son).

I get a chance to remind them, I am not getting any older, just because another year went by. I stayed 21 until I decided to turn 22, thirty years later.

> Just in case you didn't know
> Well, let me now tell you
> Birthdays are for only one reason
> With that one, make it do.
>
> A birthday is when you enter
> The world of Mom and Dad
> To lay your claim and make sure
> To tear up all they had.
>
> First, you work on the nerves
> Then you make them broke
> All your nerves they sooth
> And calm with a gentle stroke.

Diapers by the millions
Baby food by the ton
Tears by the rivers
Contentment, there seems none.

When baby is a little tot
Years, at times, seem to crawl
That is only because of over work
When the child is really small.

Ask any parent, who can tell
The years just seem to fly
Once they are big enough to help
With a vocabulary of, only why?

As teenagers, they become
You sometimes ask yourself, why?
You feel like you are crazy
And just want to go bye, bye.

Then, before you know it
Years have come and gone
What you never thought to see
A teenager is now grown.

The cycle starts all over
Someone has a birthday
Showing the grown up kid
You will now get your pay.

Birthdays should be a reminder
Every time we celebrate
No need to add another year
We're only talking of a date.

If you feel you're getting old
Remember what I said
You only have one birth day
From the day you're born 'til dead.

March 5, 1992
For Brother Ray's 56 birthday celebration

They Pierced My Sides, Too

God called me to be a Volunteer Counselor at the Pregnancy Center. Around the first of February, 2006, I heard a radio program on WFRF 105.7 Faith Radio. On the program, I heard the testimony of a young lady who had survived an abortion attempt. I knew that day that I would never be the same.

God has gotten my attention a few days earlier, when my grandson, Robert, wrote an article about a man finding a cure for the HIV virus. At the end of the story, he said that never happened, because the man was aborted and was never born.

I took my classes and learned to care for the mothers who are in crisis pregnancies. At present, I am volunteering at The Pregnancy Center of South West Georgia, in Thomasville, Georgia. This next poem was given to me by Jesus, because I could never have thought of this on my own.

It was just a tiny baby girl
In a young mother, full of fear
When I heard them say abortion
I wondered who would really care.

Tears poured down my cheeks
I stretched out my tiny arms
Reaching for someone to save me
From all this piercing and harm.

I was so small, so terribly fragile
I wasn't really able to see
But I could hear the voices
Talking of what to do with me.

I tried to get someone's attention
As saline surrounded me and my eyes burned
WHY, MOMMY? WHERE IS MY DADDY?
The answer I have never learned.

I will never know love and happiness
As other darling little girls
I was not given the chance to know
Before I was suctioned from my world.

Jesus, I know you love me
As I dance around your throne
I feel your ever loving touch
As you claimed me for your own.

I saw the scars in your hands
I saw where they pierced your side
I knew that you also suffered pain
As for my Mommy you died.

Jesus, tell my Daddy I forgive him
Just as you did from the cross
May my Mommy and my Daddy look to you
That they may not be lost.

I want to see my Mommy
I want my Daddy to hold me close
I love my Nana and my Papa
But, Jesus, I love you the most.

When I reached out for help
And tears streamed down my face
I felt the tearing of my limbs
You took me to your place.

I am safe now. I am free
I have a Father too
He reached for forty-three million babies
And handed them all to you.

October 26, 2007

What Is It Like To Be Fifty?

The next poem is written for anyone who makes it to his or her 50th birthday. The way I have seen some act when they turned forty, makes me wonder how they will make it ten more years. Every year is a blessing from God.

I really wrote this for my sister, Dee Stanley, who was born on August 14, 1944 and Betty Hunt, who was born on August 31, 1944. Happy birthday, old girls!

It is a time when everyone thinks you are getting old
Everyone, that is, except other over-fifties and yourself
It is a time when people seem to look at you strange
And every little sniffle, or sneeze means bad health.

It is a time when the skin seems to pull loose and fold
The eyes don't really see what you want them to
The ears are crammed with some invisible plugs
Before you ever get started, you find you are through.

At least, you are through remembering what you started
Of course, there is no special reason you forgot
The way you are feeling most of the time
You'd just as soon forget it as not.

For some reason, all your clothes have begun to shrink
Or else, they are making your size smaller now
Your mate tries to tell you what the problem is
But you think he is crazy anyhow.

You wake up in the morning, can't move a thing
Without feeling the bones jump off their track
Slowly, ever so slowly, you move just one leg
When you moved the other leg, you broke your back.

Your worst enemy is the mirror
You and I know just how that thing lie
If you start to prove it wrong
Somehow, it ends up making you cry.

I don't know what you are crying for
You certainly couldn't want your youth
Those teenage years were worse than now
Come on now, and just tell the truth.

You tried to wear the skirt a little shorter
But you didn't want to show your varicose veins
You tried to cut yourself some bangs
But you looked like you didn't have a brain.

Now that your feet hurt from standing so long
Your eyes have begun to swim and blur
You were certain you could make yourself younger
Oh, well, you know you are human, you did err.

So, what is it really like to be fifty?
You can take the news, it is from me
The best part of your life has just begun
If only your eyes, the truth could see.

For my sisters Dee Stanley and Betty Hunt

Happy Children's Day

I must have just discovered the new holiday called Children's Day. I don't know if it is June 11, every year, or if someone made that up. I refuse to celebrate that day. Main reason, I am always broke by the middle of the year. And, yes, that is close to the middle.

June eleven, or so they say
We celebrate Children's Day
I never knew there was a time
They didn't take my last dime.
Salvaging, screaming, vultures they be
Going to be the very death of me
Whoever thought of such a thing?
If I knew, by the neck they'd hang.
After all, how many days do they need?
Who has money after the clothes and feed?
For starters, let's name a few
Let alone the one that is new.
We have Valentine's Day for one
Then "St. Patty" and "April Fool" for fun
Easter uses up the tax money
Uncle Sam doesn't seem to think it funny.
Prom, field trips, last day of school
No wonder we parents feel like a fool
I've always heard it from the start

A fool and his money soon part.
Vacation, Fourth of July
I can't even afford to cry
Spending money must be a sin
First day of school, spending again.
Books, clothes, insurance, whoa
I don't have any more money to go
Halloween, candy for the whole nation
Rest of the week, we'll be on starvation.
Thanksgiving, we think of all we did
Count our blessings, thank God for the kid
For whom we will go straight to the store
And for Christmas, buy them more and more.
Now, what makes you think for a minute
My intentions are in it?
Children's Day indeed, I say
Just grow up and pay your own way.
But, you know how it will be
They get married, you'll see
And reward day comes at last
When their children spend just as fast.
One last word, I will say
Hope they never start Grandchildren's Day.

May 30, 1995
For all my children and of course, grandchildren too.
(It is great-grandchildren now.)

How To Keep From Getting Old

This poem, I wrote about myself, right before I turned 54. I think that was just about the time I decided to change my age from 21, to whatever age people think I am. I just love nice people. You know they are nice, when they act like they have no idea you are that old.

First, you have to determine what is old
Somewhere around a hundred, I've been told
Depending on the age of the person, you inquire
You might find it is the age you now are.
When I was just a wee little girl
My mommy was the oldest woman in the world
She was almost twenty years older than I
I was certain when I reached that age, I would lie
I knew there had to be some way to deceive
Just wasn't certain people would always believe
I thought perhaps, if I had a lot of children
I'd feel younger than I had ever been
Yeah right, keep right on dreaming
I'm getting younger everyday, it's seeming
I have six of those spending critters
Watching their budgets, gives me the jitters.
I even have a whole dozen of grand babies
A dog and a cat without rabies
When I got to the age of twenty-one
Stopping there seemed would be fun.

And so I did, and so it was
Until the rumors began to buzz
Seemed people thought I looked a bit older
To stay twenty-one, I had to get bolder.
Especially, when my child called to say
I turned the same age as you today
Well, what did I care anyhow?
My hairs have all turned gray now.
Too much of me got over there
Where the rest is, I don't care
My skin is wrinkled and dry
Keeping young, I don't even try.
I decided to grow old gracefully
Keep up with the children pacefully
Who needs to be like a teen?
Laziest product I've ever seen.
The twenties are a rough lot too
All those problems facing you
Thirties are not a whole lot better
Maybe more tired and a little fatter.
Forties, you lose weight and gain flab
Fifties are the best times for grabs
You grab this grandchild or the others
You grab time to talk with sisters and brothers
You grab your sleep between aches and pains
You grab the wheel and try to change lanes
You grab your head to try to think
Did I leave the dishes in the sink?
You grab your back before it breaks
That is enough, I've had all I can take.

January 30, 1994

Happy 53rd

Believe it or not, I do write something beside poems for Bro. Ray's birthdays. He was my pastor for 20 years. His wife, Betty, told us a lot of things about Bro. Ray and that is how I knew he didn't like getting old. He is four years older than I, and Sis. Betty is 4 years younger than I. If he ever got mad at me for making fun of his getting older, he didn't show it.

>Yeah, Brother Ray, yet another year
>About like Job, just as you feared
>Years caught up with you
>At least, that's what I heard.
>
>Some you win, some you lose
>Except the pounds, I do mean
>After forty, there is no way to compare
>The work there is, trying to stay lean.
>
>Mornings, you try to sit and dream
>Spouse thinks you are mad
>The way she keeps up the chatter
>Could make a monkey sad.
>
>Live and let live
>So, I have heard it said
>Some morning, you would be glad
>If you could drag out of bed.

Man's days are few, you see
And full of every kind of trouble
Just when you think of rest
Somebody will burst your bubble.

You know, life could be worse
Your wife could be the quiet kind
Then you would go bananas
Trying to figure out her mind.

When people talk a lot
All you have to do is listen
If you can't hear too well
Just see if the eyes are glisten.

If the eyes have a spark
It's time to have a glance
To see if your money is missing
A shopping spree on, by chance.

A man shouldn't have to worry
As I am certain you don't
When you have a talking wife
What more could you want.

Maybe a little silence
Would make your heart merry
But, remember too much quiet
Makes life too much dreary.

Come on now, just smile
Admit you have the best
Just enjoy your life now
When you are dead, you rest.

This poem is all in fun
Not to be serious in any way
Just my humorous way of
Wishing you a happy birthday.

March 8, 1989

Happy Birthday

This was written when Bro. Ray turned 54. If I calculate right, I wrote a poem for his birthday about six years in a row. I just love to tease others about getting older. You noticed I didn't say old. Years do not make us old. Years mean we just have more time to do the things we want to do for God and for others. If you stay busy and enjoy each day, you may die, but you won't be old.

I wanted to write you a poem
Can't think of anything to say
Not like most women I know
But Happy Birthday, anyway.

You may not be getting younger
In the eyes of the rest
Few people really know
The age you are, is always best.

When I was real young
I wanted to be older
When I got a little older
I just got a little bolder.

I held on to my twenty-one
And didn't let it go
When someone asks my age now
I have to subtract, to know.

I really think we have a better way
To tell how old we are
We measure it by scales or
If we can really walk that far.

If anyone would ask me
Why our age is hard to find
I just simply tell them
Age is the person's frame of mind.

Think you are old, you are
Think you are young, you see
Think all you want to
You'll never think younger than me.

The smile covers the wrinkles
The Love covers the gray
Let the world know you're young
And that's how you will stay.

Old or young, whoever you be
Make certain each and every day
To remember now, your Creator
And serve Him while you may.

March 8, 1990

Just To Prove It

February 1995, I must have felt like people thought I was getting old, and set out to prove them wrong. I'll have to say, I tried in the poem that follows.

Just to prove to you that I am not getting old
I'll just for once, do as I am told
If that doesn't prove I am a teenager
I'll give you all of my wager.

I will do better than that for you
I'll turn off the light when I am through
I'll wipe my feet before entering the door
That should knock you through the floor.

Just to prove to you that I am young still
I'll show you, yes sir, I really will
I can act just like a silly teen
Look in the mirror, thinking I am a queen.

I can put on that war paint, with the best
Look like a clown, just like the rest
I can wear my dresses short, skimpy and tight
Never mind, that I don't look too bright.

I can curl my hair, or string it into my face
I can look like something from out of space
I could listen to that terrible rock beat
Until I am so crazy I think I am neat.

I got to have me a car, so I can be independent
Now I know where all of my parents' money went
I know everything, you can't tell me nothing
Only thing I can hear is a telephone ring.

Don't you think I am acting more youthful each day?
Walking and swinging my head every which way
Some of the things I watch on TV
Make me even wonder about me.

I am very cool, maybe even very smart
If only, I could have known from the start
That I am only as old as I feel
I'd have known life is really real.

Not the life of a teenager anyway
Just listen to what I have to say
The time when life could be at its best
But I am like all the rest.

Don't realize I need a lot of guidance
Therefore, I don't use my common sense
Common sense would quickly tell me
To open up my pretty eyes and see.

That others have gone this path before
And haven't a chance to cross once more
Common sense would tell me to watch their mistake
I know what I am doing, the same one I will make.

I'll have you to know, I'm in my youth
I can't help, but tell you the truth
You know I am young and will never be old
Because, this teenager does just as she is told.

Date Unknown

You Know I Will

Sometimes, I will be in the mood to write a poem, or maybe, I am trying to write. What ever it be, I can't think of a lot to say that sounds right. This was one of those times. I think I was doing the family Newsletter and wanted to make the fourth page.

You thought I forgot to write
A verse, or two, for fun
But, just as always in the past
I dug down and got one.

One what? Oh, yes, a verse
You think I'm a bit senile
I'll prove it, if you sit
And listen for a little while.

What am I trying to prove?
Now, for the very life of me
I don't know what it is
Nor what it could really be.

I closed my blood-shot eyes
Propped up my double chin
I tied a towel around my head
Trying to remember once again.

I looked an awful sight
As Woody popped through the door
Now, I knew what I forgot
Didn't need to think any more.

I opened my weary eyes
Untied my aching head
That can't be what I dug for
So, I went off to bed.

September 19, 1992

A View From The Pew

With this poem, I am thinking about the people who attend churches. I have been in many churches in my lifetime. I have seen and heard a lot of things. I am not certain what prompted me to write this one, but I am sure someone got me upset. I may not say anything, but I can certainly put my feelings on paper, and then forget what I was mad about.

Ask any old lady, child, or gent
How many hours have been spent
Sitting on the old church pews
Interesting to hear all those views.

Whose work are we promoting?
Just do it, never mind voting
Who cares what pew dwellers think?
Keep quiet, never mind your rank.

Can't please everyone all the time
To please anyone, seems a crime
Why should pew dwellers be concerned?
When, by their actions, they seem unlearned.

Unless you are experienced, really
You may find yourself a dilly
One person having all the say
While others just pay and pay.

We hear talk of love and care
Who really loves, or even dare?
Just when you feel you can trust
Be on guard, you feel you must.

What will be said, and about who?
Maybe him, her, me, or you
Your name, not likely to be spoken
You are being put down, and no joking.

Though you sit on a pew
With every right to have a view
Be careful what you hear and see
Be clear in mind, what you'll be.

When at the judgment you stand
Will blood be dripping from your hands
Of those you failed to lift
When once you saw them start to drift?

You saw them leave one by one
You knew the hurt that was done
Not one word did you dare say
As quietly a soul walked away.

It was agreed, not worth keeping
Thrown away without any weeping
How many more will I view
As I sit lamely in my pew?

December 27, 1991

What Makes a Good Family Reunion?

What is your favorite time of the year? Some will say it is Christmas, Easter, or maybe the Fourth of July. My favorite time is family reunion. Our family has our reunion every third Saturday in August. We usually start on Friday night, with a cookout. This is for the people who make it early. I am always one of that bunch. Saturday is the big day, when we have more food on the table than an Army mess hall. We eat, talk, laugh, and have a ball. We even have some fussing and fighting. That is how we know we are kin. Anyway, let the party begin.

I wanted to write about the ingredients for family reunion
But didn't know where to begin
Then, I thought, oh well, just pick a good time and place
And watch for all the kin.

Mom is already right there at home, scratching and digging
Raking up all those pots and kettles
If you search around the kitchen, there's food of every kind
But keep your cotton-picking fingers out of the vittles

Every year, you can look for the people, as one by one they come
Some as close as next door, as they prance right in
Others as far away as Florida. Yeah, we got to look at
That crazy bunch again.

Barbara gets there just in time for dinner
But she brings a big box with a lot of stuff
That stuff is for the after dinner fun time
When name drawing makes a lot of us feel rough.

Rough, if it is something we want and our name isn't drawn
You just smile and act real cool
Although you have eaten so much, a little fast too
About all you can do now is drool.

Now, believe me, that isn't all the people you will have around
There's plenty more, to be sure
You have the preacher and his nice little wife, Brenda
Their off-springs make six more.

From North Carolina we have a clown. Surely, you know his name
Junior, come on in and sit down
Now, I started something I may not be able to fit on the roll
The names of all who think they are clowns.

If you can't make a rhyme, you are just out of luck
And, you may be a number, but have no fear
North Carolina has more to offer as you shall soon see
When Bonnie and Amos both get here.

Well, lo and behold, and bless my soul
I forgot Clarence, Phillip and old Randall too
There's Sherry, Derrick, Candice, and no other but Kim
Poor Rocki and Scott, I nearly forgot you.

Let's hear one for Virginia, spread through the roving hills
Are John Boy with all her crew
Rebekah, Lisa, James, and all of their little ones
With Chris and Tina makes for a few.

Randy has four, Angie, Eric, Pam and Chris, increases the list
Furr and Bud are just a few miles away
While Michael, Cynthia and boys add another four
With Wilma, Jerry and Shannon, what shall I say?

I could say that is all, but you know much better
Kevin lives on the ridge alone
Debbie, Buster, and Tonya have a mansion on the hill
But don't expect me to go on and on.

Ambrosia and Michael live down by Tampa Bay
Pat and Woody dwell down in the woods
Charity, Duane, Trish and Buddy, will arrive before long
Teresa and Alicia, I'd bring if I could.

The ones I have named, you will plainly see
We will have others there as well
We will bring the memories in our hearts and mind
Although the loneliness we can not tell.

July 26, 1996

Writing

The fourth of July, 1991, found me up late, trying to write a poem. Seems that Charity is making noise, and disturbing me. It must have been bad, because I didn't get much written before I called it quits. Charity loves to read half the night, and is usually lost in a book. Otherwise, don't try to think around her. Especially when she was at the age of fifteen.

>Here I sit
>Late at night
>Raking my brain
>Trying to write.
>
>Must be some way
>To keep my kid quiet
>So my brain is at ease
>As I continue to write.
>
>Husband already asleep
>All snuggled up tight
>Dreaming of his bunny
>As she still tries to write.
>
>With all my heart
>With all my might
>I love to eat
>But not more than write.
>
>*July 4, 1991*

All In A Pastor's Day

In June, 2005, Rev. James Lott had been our pastor for five years. We had a celebration for the occasion. Sister Elaine, was in charge of the program, and asked if I would like to say something. Of course, I did, and the following poem was created, sometime that week. Forgot the date I wrote the next poem.

"Want to say something?" Sister Elaine, asked
Speaking of Brother Lott's fifth anniversary day
Right up my alley, and just my speed
Always got something intelligent to say.

I remember the first time I saw him
Almost late for his pastoral interview
Couldn't find Boston Church of God
Don't think he had a clue.

He didn't have a clue who we are
Nor how difficult we can be
But if you check his gray hairs
You won't have to believe me.

I know half of his problems
They are my own family
The other half, you'll find
Are just friends to me.

He thinks I am trying to boss him
When I suggest what he should do
I think he talks too much to my crew
He's beginning to act like them too.

I am old enough to be his grandmother
And wise enough to treat him kind
Believe me, when I act too wise
I get a piece of his mind.

He keeps talking about his crew
How they keep him on the go
I really think it is Sister Jennifer
Who keeps him on his toes.

Every time I talk to her
He wants to know what we are scheming
If he thinks we are going to tell
He must be really dreaming.

I watch Cody, that little chip
When he gets all angry and pout
In my mind, I see his Daddy
And wonder why his Mom didn't knock him out.

I almost forgot I am supposed to be serious
We are celebrating his "special day"
I am just as serious as I know how to be
But I have plenty more to say.

I say, you should put locks on the sanctuary doors
Like the ones you have at home
Than the people couldn't escape
Up and down the halls to roam.

He knows what I am talking about
You enter the room and shut the door
It can only be opened from the other side
Do I have to tell you more?

Well, I'll tell you one thing
If I had him there, when I dug out
He would have left faster than he came
If he had to make a new route.

Sometimes, he comes to our house
To feast upon a home cooked meal
He knows more about cooking than I
I can't believe, he is for real.

I think we have come to grips
He can't tell me a thing
After all is said and done
I am just like the rest of the gang.

Put all kidding aside, if I may
Bro. Lott is the very best
So treat him nice and with love
I think he has passed our test.

There is another important test
This one is for you and me
To be as good a member
As we want, our Pastor to be.

Don't know how much time I am allowed
To tell all the Pastor's trash
But, for the sake of being nice
I will shut up, and make a dash.

June 2005

SECTION THREE

This section has an assortment of poems. There are sixteen of them. They were written at times when I have been very troubled about a situation, or when I was just trying to be funny. My mood can change in a heartbeat, but that is the right of every woman. The poems in this section were written over a period of several years. All of them will allow you to get into my thoughts and feelings.

I want you to enjoy reading as much as I enjoy writing for you. I know that some of you may even be able to relate to some of these poems. I am certain I am not the only person to feel the pains and heartaches of life, and what it has to offer at times. But, along with every burden, is always the love of God to give us strength and help us make it another day.

Just Wondering

The following poem was written on November 25, 1993. It was only three days after Wanda would have been 55 years old, had she not died in June, the same year. I don't have to tell you her death made an impact on my life. She was only 15 months older than I. She was my oldest sister. When she was a baby, she fell off the bed and nearly died. We think that was the reason she was never able to talk plainly. She always walked with a limp. There were things about her that made me realize that she would have been a very smart person, had she not been without oxygen for a few minutes after the fall. We didn't have all the modern technology of today, else things could have been different. I will always wonder.

> I can not see beyond the horizon
> To that country across the way
> I just have to let myself wonder
> What it will be like someday.
>
> Of the future, I visualize
> While of old times reminiscing
> Heaven unfolds before me
> My thoughts are so convincing.
>
> Daddy, is that you by the river
> Sitting 'neath the tree of life?
> Did you go to meet Wanda
> When she left this world of strife?

I see you Wanda, strolling among the flowers
I saw you touch the pretty rose
Can you see, I long to be there?
I guess, only God knows.

Randy, you came with Daddy
As he met her at the gate
So long since you saw her
Guess you could hardly wait.

Did Wanda tell each of you
How long I waited at her bed
Just to hear her speak to me?
A farewell, she never once said.

You can't imagine how hard it is
To want someone to stay
While, at the same time
You know they are going away.

If only, I kept telling myself
I knew that she could hear me
As I told her how I cared
How I wanted her to see.

Her eyes remained closed
No words did she speak
Hours became mixed with others
As all seemed so bleak.

As the three of you sit together
And you remember us here
Ask God to please send Jesus
To take us to be there

November 25, 1993

God's Footstool

I entered a poetry contest with the following poem. I don't think they had a clue that I was writing a poem about West Virginia and calling those hills God's footstool.

In the days of mighty creation
As God was drawing a blueprint
Carefully laying out the plans
Beauty is what I think He meant.

So splendidly He designed her
This state in all her wonder
Mountains full of wild rhododendron
Placed in the Appalachian yonder.

Where the cardinals perch and sing
Atop the coal filled hill
Men and women praise a God
As here, you know He is real.

Real indeed, you have to say
As you view afar mountains blue
Smelling the freshness of dawn
As the sun's rays come marching thru.

God has a throne in Heaven
He needed a place to rest His feet
He choose it, there in West Virginia
Where time and eternity meet.

September 20, 1989

Finishing Touch

Not certain just when I wrote the next poem. Not even certain, why I wrote it. But I think I was mad at Woody for some reason. I always thought men did not appreciate women and their God-given abilities to take care of man. Of course, I am not a man, and do not know what makes him tick, but I know God knew he would be hopeless and helpless without someone to look after him. So, God created Eve.

God drew up his blueprint
His plans were all laid out
That God knew what He was doing
I have not even a little doubt.

Look at the sun, hanging in space
The stars fill the whole sky
The moon in all its true charm
Kisses the velvet, night goodbye.

Mountains, taller than I can see
Covered by chilly ice and snow
While in the valley far below
Gardens have begun to grow.

Who, other than our God,
Could make a world so grand?
Where mighty ocean tides
Beat upon white silver sand?

God formed all the winged fowls
To the animals, he gave sweet life
But not one was quite suitable
To become Adam's special wife.

Adam was created from just clay
Made in the image of He
Placed there in the garden
From cares he was most free.

He was lonely, things were quiet
God knew his every increasing need
Put him to sleep. Take out a rib.
Break his silence, yes indeed.

You'd think man would be grateful
For his helper, God to him gave.
But each time she makes a move
By habit, he rants and rave.

God wanted Adam to be happy
All of his needs to be met
Bound up in the bones of woman
Best of God's creation yet.

Date Unknown

How To Remodel Your House

We lived in an old doublewide that Woody's Dad had given to us. It was well built when it was new, but it was getting old and in need of some repairs. I can paint and wallpaper any old day I take a notion. I could have built a house with all the work I put into the make-over. After I got all the fixing-up done, there was no way I was letting anyone get a speck of dirt on anything. I barked the orders and laid down the rules. The kids wished I had just let the place fall down, because now they had to take their shoes off, just to enter the house.

First, you take a look around
Notice the sink is falling down
Decide to buy one that is new
Need cabinets, but not a few.

Once you have them in place
You notice all the storage space
Overhead, old cabinets look rough
No money for new, so that is tough.

Wallpaper, the name of the game
Old cabinets never look the same
Floors must have a new look
Kitchen to clean now, to cook.

Now, look at the rest of the house
Look at the kids and your spouse
Let them know the new law
Dirtiest bunch you ever saw.

Now, this house must get clean
Tired of these carpets of green
Ruby is the color, quite bold
Put it down, the men were told.

Make it Teal, for the bedroom
Too much Ruby, would be my doom
Now take of your shoes, you critters
By now, they all have the jitters.

Don't put anything out of place
Or I'll send you to outer space
Throw everything old out
We'll get new, without a doubt.

Leave Woody right where he sits
I didn't say he was to get
Now here we sit, all alone
Where have all the children gone?

A home to clean is no fun
Continually scrubbing, till day is done
Don't sit here and don't eat there
Make a mess, don't you even dare.

I think I'll let up a tad
To find some dirt, I will be glad
I'll know the kids have crept in
And I'll start scolding them again.

There is a difference in a house and a home
A home is where you live, a house you roam
Come on kids, lets live awhile
Kick off your shoes and start to smile.

You know you like it, spic and span
Come on now, enjoy it while you can
Soon you'll grow up and have a home
You'll like it better. A house you roam.

July 26, 1994

Will You Cast Me Aside, Lord?

I do not know when this poem was written. Don't know if I had a dream and was disturbed, or if I thought it in my mind. One day, I found the poem on my computer. I knew it was about a little girl who attended my church. The congregation was to give approval for three children to be asked not to come back to our church. I knew in my heart this was not right, but I didn't speak in their defense. I vowed never again would I sit quiet. I prayed God, forgive me.

I stood in the judgment of God, with my head bowed low
I could hear as He judged the ones before
Ere, He asked of each one's deed
Whom had they helped in the time of need?

I knew He would ask me the same questions
I shifted endlessly in my position
Maybe, I would find some way to explain
When the question is asked again.

I'd tell Him how busy I had been
I never really thought about it then
When the test was put before me
I knew I had to choose, you see.

She was only a little child
Not once had I ever seen her smile
Deep within her heart of threads
Though torn in pieces, was lead.

So heavy, for one so small
No mother answered, when she calls
Left alone to face the world
Mother had betrayed this little girl.

As I stood there at the judgment
My waiting time nearly spent
She wouldn't leave my mind
What had I done, so unkind?

I was doing what was my duty
At least, I knew it had to be
We could not let her ruin our place
And bring to our church a disgrace.

Our children might be lead astray
By this sad child of disarray
We could just ask her to leave
Who would be hurt, or grieve?

I listened close, I barely heard
The most dreaded of words
Depart from me, I know you not.
Oh, God, will this be my lot?

She had become a cast-away
Bound by that long ago day
As ones, she thought were a friend
Made of her welcome, an end.

With no mom, no church, no hope
She turned to the world and dope
Forever doomed, she will be
Because of people just like me.

I could have spoken in her defense
But didn't use my common sense
I left it up to others to speak
As I sat quiet and meek.

I had many reasons for why
To tell you now, I'll try
I was hurt many times before
I just said, not any more.

Then it was my time to hear
As trembling with fear
I walked before the throne
As our God sat thereon.

I knew the question He would ask
I hurriedly explained my task
I chose not to stand for right
Since God understood my plight.

Oh, God, another chance, I plead
I'll defend the person in need
Of one to love and care
Away with all my fear.

I knew it was too late to plead
A soul had been lost indeed
I screamed, God, hear my cry
As I realized the lost was I.

Awaking to sounds of grief
I felt a joyful relief
Another chance, I now had
You can believe, I was glad.

When I stand before His throne
He will claim me as His own
That one who needs a friend
I will hold in my own hands.

I'll not fear what anyone thinks
Matters not, what their ranks
It's the Master that holds the key
To unlock fear, and set me free.

Date Unknown

What Mama Knew

I was asked to write a poem to be read at a Mother-Daughter Brunch for Mothers Day at the Boston Church of God. I asked God what I should write and the following poem is what I wrote.

>I remember, many years ago
>While I was just a child
>Some days, I were an angel
>Others, I were just wild.
>
>Wild about this boy
>Wild about that one
>Infatuation was wonderful
>But, not really much fun.
>
>Mama knew me so well
>My mind, I knew she could read
>When I was into my own plans
>I'd hear, "You had better take heed."
>
>I could always count on Mama
>To wreck my every wonderful scheme
>She had eyes on every side of her head
>Or, so for me it seemed.

I could get into more trouble
And I didn't even try
Mostly, when she said "don't"
I always had to ask "why?"

As I got older and I ask "why?"
I got a lesson of the day
When she quoted the Bible
And said, "You do it God's way."

I knew it was settled
She wasn't playing any game
If I wanted to be just like her
I had to do the same.

I listened, and I learned well
How to keep one step ahead
How crazy can one child be?
It's a wonder that I ain't dead.

She gave me all the instruction
Of just how I should live
When I became a Mama
It was my turn to give.

I did give to every child
All the instruction I had learned
A Master's degree in parenting
I knew I had earned.

What you sow, is what you reap
Each child was just like me
A whole new ball game of life
What is to be will be.

Whether it was to be, or not
I didn't have to read their mind
All I had to do was remember
And I knew this kind.

The kind that seeks their own way
No matter what they have been told
To tell you the honest truth
I was never that bold.

I learned from my Mama
Just what I should do
So, down on my knees alone
I prayed, Lord, I give them to you.

What a gift to give to God
As we place each child in His arms
And know without a doubt
He can keep them from harm.

Have we so soon forgotten
The things that Mama knew
Of how to raise our children
And teach them what to do?

We owe it to our children
To pray for them each day
And, with the Bible, guide them
That they too will know the way.

There is a way that seems right
But the end thereof is destruction
Could this be the very reason
There is such a distraction?

A distraction from the Word
A distraction from prayers
If Mama doesn't teach the way
Then tell me who really cares.

Young lady, as you start your home
And children are placed in your care
Just remember what Mama knew
The love of God to always share.

You may be very young
You may be very old
But, you will never go wrong
If you heed what the Word has told.

Now, Mama is in heaven
She no longer fills her pew
The task now, of teaching children
Is left up to me and you.

I will do my part
You can do yours
To take our generation
To heaven's fair shores.

That is the reason
He has placed us here
So we may reach out to God
As He, in His love, draws near.

Now, if you want to know
What my Mama knew
Just take the old Bible
And read it through.

Follow all the instructions
As from your heart you pray
Teach it to your children
And show them the way.

And someday in sweet heaven
As you meet your children there
You will hear, "Thank you for the Bible
And thank you for your prayers."

May 6, 2006

Time Goes On

I have done a monthly Newsletter for my family for a long time. I always try to include a poem for the fourth page. This is one of those times I was just thinking.

I sit and strain my mind, wiggle my nose and pull my hair
Just trying to think of something to write for a rhyme
After a while, I grow blank and my eyes start to stare
About then, my mind goes back into time.

You know what I mean by back, back when?
When you and I were just young whelps
Life was slow and carefree and then
We grew up and screamed for help.

Seems you and I never knew life wasn't fair
Although we must have sensed as much
Growing up, we would never so much as dare
To denounce life, and think of such.

Oh, yeah, we screamed, "Ain't no fair"
If we didn't get our own way
When really, we didn't have a care
We knew not of more grown up days.

Did you hear what the child said?
Once sounded like you and I
Not wanting to go to bed
Kissing the playful day good bye.

Time passes on, as we both know
Soon it will be their time
To wonder where did time go
And what happen to my last dime.

History repeats itself, they say
We grew up and screamed for help
Now dawns a new, but same day
We hear it from our own whelps.

So life goes on, and so we dream
Of time, when history closes
And from our life we will gleam
Foot prints there, among the roses.

July 29, 1995

Computers

I love and am amazed by computers. To think I was scared to death the first time I turned one on. I was afraid it would blow up. When it didn't blow up in my face, I had it mastered. I learned computer programming when I was in Thomas Tech. I associate a computer with the mind of a man. When you know what's inside, you win.

Now, everyone knows what a computer is
Or, is it really what you always thought?
I am the all knowledge one, right now
And, tell you all, I know I ought!

I know I ought to just let you learn for yourself
And when I am finished, you'll agree
Shall I continue? Tell me yes, or no
Yes, you say. Get ready for a spree.

I got to thinking about this trap
Because a trap is sometimes what it seems
I get bogged down in some menu or other
And can't even get it out of my dreams.

It seems the trap thinks I am crazy
If I click to exit the document
The idiot always says, Are you sure?
Other times, I know not where it even went.

I tried to delete one of my files
The Lord knew I didn't know how
There didn't seem to be any way
Until I called on my old pal.

Bobby Lee seems to know a lot
Probably, a lot of that is bluff
But he got the book and started to read
Soon, I was rid of all that stuff.

I can read as good as he can
But I have a mouse to consider
When you try to read, and move a mouse
You want to break the crazy critter.

There is nothing I don't know now
Don't think I am some kind of a clown
When I have had all I can take
I simply shut the trap down.

June 30, 1997
It's shut-down time again.

'Twas The Day After Thanksgiving

This one was written before Thanksgiving ever got here in 1997. But I know how it is, every year, on the day after the holiday. That is when the Christmas shopping really starts. Early in the morning, before daylight, the people line up at the front of the stores, ready to grab the bargains. People have been pushed down and badly hurt in all the confusion of trying to be the first in the store. Once when I dropped Charity off at Wal-Mart for her job, the women begin to jump out of the cars and come running, because they thought she was going to beat them into the store. It was 4:00 A.M. and you would think all these people would be home asleep.

'Twas the day after Thanksgiving, in the land of the free
Where all the people were scrambling just trying to be
   A little richer than the folks living next door
   I can't understand whatever they grab for.

   Shooting and killing seems only for thrills
   Lives, it seems, are taken at anyone's will
   Each person living within the four walls
   Caring not that his neighbors may fall.

Fall, yes surely, from grace he could
Blindly, he stumbles, not knowing he would
Be more blessed, living in a tent
Then, in a mansion, though short of the rent.

Now, we know Christmas is surely near
Since it comes to us once each year
So, why all the rumbling and fuss?
Buying all those gifts, we must.

Already forgotten is yesterday's meal
When we sat and ate to our fill
Not even the blessing, most people ask
Being thankful is not their daily task.

If God gave gifts according to our gratitude
Most of us would change our attitude
Else, we would just find ourselves without
Complaining to God, there is no doubt.

We need not worry. We need not fret
Devil hasn't taken all our blessings yet
This Christmas, let's do it right
Thank God at morning, noon and night.

Show God, He's worthy of our praise
As together, our voices we raise
In honor to God's dear Son
Because He is truly the Only One.

October 31, 1997

The ABC's Of Living

Once, I gave a little sermon, called the ABC's of living. It was well liked by several people. Later, I decided to make a poem out of it. A poem relays some type of message, good or bad, most of the time.

Always be yourself
Be sure to smile
Count all your blessings
Daydream a little while.

Eat a balanced diet
Faithful in every way
Grateful to your friends
Help someone every day.

Ignore all evil temptations
Joy in your salvation
Kindness, show to everyone
Love all God's creation.

Make a joyful noise unto the Lord
Never try, people to be pleasing
Obey the commands of God
Pray without ceasing.

Quit God, don't dare
Righteousness will prevail
Satan hates holiness
Tongues of evil will fail.

Utter not a word of doubt
Victory comes in the morning
Wonder no more alone
Exclaim the holy warning.

Yearn for the kingdom
Zion must travail
Until this life is finished
With God, all will be well.

July 2, 1991

How Will It Be?

This poem was written while thinking of the shortness of time in this life. I will soon be fifty-four, at the time I wrote this. It seemed, just a short time ago, I was a child.

I suppose not any of us like a lot of questions
Although most of us receive them a lot
We don't have to give an answer, except for IRS
There is someone else, you can believe or not.

I am no different from the rest of you
When it comes to trying to give my best
After we have given our answer so well
Our life will really tell the rest.

Not to far distant time over beyond
We'll stand with all of God's creation
The words will sound loud and clear
What did you do with thy Salvation?

Everything seems so important to us
As we race madly from here to there
Everything that is, except soul matters
Why don't most people seem to care?

There are those who say they have died
When they arrived, all around was light
They don't mind telling you
In this life, nothing was made right.

How long will man be deceived?
And look for the easy way out?
When God gave His very best, and
Jesus paved a straight and narrow route.

How will you find this Salvation
About which God will soon ask you?
The answer is in His Holy Word
I ask, "What are you going to do?"

When I ask myself a lot of questions
As I examine my own life
I realize we are so helpless
Living in a world full of strife.

I just look up to my Jesus
And place my life in His care
When I am asked, "where is thy Salvation?"
I'll look to Jesus, standing there.

January 7, 1994

Forever Spring

There are times when I write a poem, and looking back, do not remember the reason it was written. I have been told that I am "too heavenly minded, to be any earthly good." That is because I am always talking about heaven and what it will be like to just get home. Home is where the heart is. I guess this poem is reminiscing.

In the spring, when flowers are budding
Young hearts are all a fluttering
Little gals dressed in their finery
The young men, sweet words are uttering.

Youth, in all their swinging array
Seem to notice not the time
As on and on the hands turn
Until the aging clock must chime.

Oh, little gal, where is your frock?
Placed in some cedar storage space
Waiting for one spring day soon
When your granddaughter, it will grace.

How many springs have come and gone
Since that night, so long ago?
Too many for the heart to ponder
Really, she doesn't want to know.

Her lover has a long time been gone
Waiting in the forever spring
When once again as they meet
Their youthful voices will sing.

Each day she waits and longs
As she watches another setting sun
She looks beyond the crimson glow
Knowing soon, her journey will be done.

One spring morning, she did not awake
During the night, she slipped away
To join her lover of yester years
Where all is spring and ever day.

February 14, 1994

Time Goes On

This next poem was written for a Newsletter. When you write a Newsletter every month and try to have a new poem, you sometimes have to write when nothing is in the head to come out. However, time goes on, and I will write something before the deadline.

You didn't think I would, or maybe you didn't think I could.
    But, as sure as I sit here tonight,
    About my birthday, I will write.
    Not every day we turn sixty-two,
    But here I am, how about you?
    Yesterday, I was just twenty-one,
    Life was great and full of fun.
    Today, the years have come and gone,
    Life is speedily moving along.
    Gray hair replaces the once brown,
    Thinning strands expose my crown.
    The skin on my head I mean,
    And my body is no longer lean.
    I guess we are blessed with poor sight,
    We can't see all the wrinkles we fight.
    The hearing is also getting bad,
    If it wasn't, we'd probably be sad.
    To hear all the things people say,
    Because I am old and "set in my ways."
    When I kneel, I can't stand again,

I feel like the bones will just cave in.
I wonder who will care for me tomorrow,
When life is frail and full of sorrow.
I think of my children, and know they would;
But being older than I, don't think they could.
The grandchildren are so slow,
I'd be gone and they wouldn't know.
Those critters live in their own land,
Before me, they will be on a cane.
I've known it all my life,
So don't need all your strife.
Age is just a thought in the mind,
And I'll have none of the kind.
I'll always be young in heart and soul,
And set for me, my own goal.
To always smile, no matter the pain,
To act like I am young again.
Always be busy, helping someone.
Eventually, when my days are done
They'll walk by my coffin and say,
"She never looked as young as today."
Don't think I can't hear your mind,
So let all your words be real kind.
Don't think I can't see you too,
So just be nice, whatever you do.
To the children and grands I leave,
Don't worry when you see them grieve.
They are only wondering what they'll do,
With no one to tell them how to.

February 18, 2002

I Need A Valentine

Looking back over this poem to see why I wrote it makes me wonder the reason. But I think I was mad at my husband, for some reason or the other. I don't know if he was complaining because I didn't get him a valentine, or if he was complaining because no one got a valentine for him to give me. I think I was just a little mad with him, because he was complaining about something.

> I know Woody isn't getting me a Valentine
> The poor man doesn't even have a dime
> I could loan him a few bucks
> But he would loose them, with his lucks.
>
> He tried to whisper in my ear
> Doesn't know, I can't even hear
> "Read my lips," I heard him say
> "What's wrong with you, anyway?"
>
> When you get old, your steps are slow
> A lot you don't want others to know
> Guess that is why, we become a grouch
> Can hardly move off the couch.
>
> Complain, complain, must be your middle name
> What is your first? Well, it's the same
> Everyone I guess has a last
> "What is yours?" Tell me fast.

Ole, slow, grouchy thing
There you did it again
Asked you a question very nice
Don't think, I'll repeat it twice.

But if you will perk up your ears
Once in the next several years
You will hear me call your name again
As I shout, Complain, Complain, Complain!

I wrote this to my sweet hubby
You might quote it to your Bubby
Of course, the argument that pursue
Won't start with me or you.

So I will tell you ahead of time
Better scrounge up a dime
Might take more than a few
To do what you must do.

Run out and get a Valentine
Make sure it looks real fine
Send it to the old, sweet boy
Fill his gizzard with pure joy.

February 7, 2000

Holiday Woes

This was the first Christmas since my Mother died in June, 1999. I wanted to get away from home for the holidays. Woody and I went to Macon, Georgia, and got a motel. I had been sick since Mom died. Even though I went to the motel just to rest, I certainly didn't get any rest. I was very sick and could hardly get out of bed. When I was able, I got my stuff together and headed home.

>Holidays nearly got me down
>Spent two days and nights in my gown
>Didn't know what was so wrong
>Just seemed to last too long.
>
>First, my left collar bone hurt
>Probably because it's made of dirt
>Upset stomach all Christmas Eve
>Too sick to stay, to sick to leave.
>
>I was in a motel for much needed rest
>That is not what I do best
>I wanted it to be peaceful and quiet
>With Woody around, yeah right.
>
>I missed the phone calls
>Wanted to know "How are you alls?"
>While four days went by
>Only two people said "Hi."

I wouldn't dare confess the truth
Really, no one has the proof
But it's been in my thought
Confess, I know I ought.

I missed my girls
The best in all the worlds
I missed my boys too
I think I missed the rest of you.

Finally, I packed all my junk
Threw it all in the trunk
Going home, I was fine
Sickness, I had left behind.

January 13, 2000

I Am Sixty-Three

For someone that doesn't claim to be old, I certainly do write a lot of poetry about old age. Anyway, it is a lot better to be getting older, because there is only one other choice. I want to go to heaven, but my girls won't give me permission to leave now.

Not everyone can boast of being as old as I
Nor can they sift through their brains
And find all the grit and grins
That makes up our earthly gains.

To some, life is a great burden
To others, it is just a pure joy
For most, I now realize
The enemy sneaks along to destroy.

Life is just what you make it
I have often been told
Mine is just what God made of it
That is why I have lived to be old.

Now, I know you wouldn't blame God
If you made such a mess as mine
But I am giving God the credit
For with my life, He does just fine.

I doubt that I would be here
If it were not for my King
I would be lost in utter despair
And not possess anything.

Life is really worth the living
And you can live it to the fullest
If you lend a helping hand, as
To others, you will do your best.

Every day may not be a rose
It certainly won't be a weed
If you honor God's plan for you
And the Bible you will heed.

Getting old is wonderful
Getting old is kind of grand
When you take all your friends
And enter heaven hand in hand.

March 12, 2003

SECTION FOUR

Section four contains nineteen poems. They are all written at different times and for different occasions. Some, I suppose, are a little funny. Some are a little serious, but all are from my heart or mind. I think you will be able to tell the difference. Some people think there is not a serious bone in my whole body. That is debatable, but I am not going to debate it in this book.

'Twas Two Weeks Before Christmas

The following poem was written for a group of people I worked with at NETS. I was a bookkeeper.

'Twas two weeks before Christmas, throughout all NETS
Wagging and dragging, just acting like vets
The children were nestled all snuggled in class
Teachers all wondering, how long will this last?

Monthly meeting was over, the goals had been set
The visions of two weeks, they were going to get
Kept roaming the mind, refusing to leave
So much idle time, makes a bookkeeper just grieve.

Dr. Art, and old Scrooge, locked behind the door
Hiding all the money, and calling for more
Dr. Les had some pity, said "bring the bucks in"
Just like always, they sat there and grin.

When's payday? Someday, just wait and see
Had you been working hard, you'd forget it, like me
My teachers need pay, our participants too
Tell us the reason, can't get money from you.

I know you think I am scrooge, so tight I squeak
If it wasn't for money, Lindsey would never speak
Ole, Burnett does her share, screaming for the green
Those two beat all I have ever seen.

Speaking of green, the color I like best
Around this place, I fit with the rest
It's simply amazing, the reasons they find
To get all the money. Just blows my mind.

Oh, the phone is ringing, it's for Gwen
Don't tell me, a man is calling again
You're lucky ole girl, you get the call
With the flirt around, she likes them all.

I've heard it said and you have too
Can't run with the big dogs; know what you can do?
Just stay on the porch, soak up the sun
While others are running, having the fun.

Life is a joy, when you work at NETS
Count all your blessings, cursing forget
You know when all is said and done
You're special at NETS, every last one.

Oh, yes, the last one, James the name
We'd all like to say we're glad you came
You can reinforce the accounting place
Make certain all reports don't have a blank space.

I searched and I searched trying to find
Some reason to believe, I still have a mind
Only thing to do was to convince myself
There's plenty of mind, not enough wealth.

I devised a plan, put it under lock and key
MANAGERS make the money bring it to me
I promise you one thing, that is for sure
You haven't gotten much, you won't get much more.

Forget you, Janet? not in a million years
If it wasn't for you, I might realize my fears
That Lindsey wouldn't have reasons for money to ask
As long as you're here, writing checks will be my task.

Caroline writes your paychecks, I know you are delighted.
If I had to write them, most of you would be slighted.
Not because I don't love and wish you well
It just doesn't take money, my greetings to tell.

We've had a good time throughout the days
Other times, believe me, we prays and prays
Merry Christmas to all and a Happy New Year.
If you don't need any money, I'll be right here.

December 4, 1987

The Way To Eternal Happiness

I am not certain when I wrote the first part of this poem, but the last three verses were written much later on May 3, 2004. The way to eternal happiness is not found in ways that we sometimes think. We think if we have money, we will be happy. Or, we may think poverty will make us sad. It depends on which side of the river of life you are on. This world is not the end at all. This world is only the dressing room. You can put on the robe of your choice. Chose life in Christ and live forever, or chose the riches of this world and leave it all here on earth.

The story is told by Jesus, our Lord
Of a rich man who faired sumptuously
While a beggar lay at his gate
I wonder if he could hear his pleas.

Lazarus only desired the crumbs from his table
As the dogs came and licked his sores
No doubt the wealthy, as they passed him there
Thought of Lazarus as just a bore.

One day, it happened as appointed to man
The death angel came knocking at his door
Life on earth was over now
Cries from Lazarus, he would hear no more.

Into the bosom of Father Abraham
Lazarus was carried by the angel, you see
When we choose the ways of God
There'll be an angel for you and me.

As the story relates, there is more to hear
Of a rich man, raising his eyes in hell
Realizing his riches were left behind,
As were his five brothers as well.

Father Abraham reminded the poor, rich man
While on earth, he had his good day
While the wages of sin is always death
God never forgets to give each his pay.

If you are a rich man in this world
In your riches, please don't trust
Lay up your treasures in heaven
Where they neither, decay, or rust.

Date Unknown

He'll Be There

This poem was written a long time ago on March 14, 1989. Sometimes, I am sitting around, and just decide to write a poem. Or, I may be driving and have to stop to write the title and a few lines so I don't forget what I am writing about. I don't consider myself a super Christian, but I certainly serve a Super God. He is my everything! As long as I know He is on the throne, all is well. I know He is on the throne and that is why the devil is on earth bothering us. My confidence is in God.

> He'll be there when you are lonely
> Not a friend can be found
> He'll be right by your side
> He'll help you to abound.
>
> Trials come to each of us
> As it did to Jacob of old
> But you will find an answer
> If to His hand you will hold.
>
> Death somehow finds his way
> Right through your open door
> Leaving you to feel the loser
> Thinking joy will be no more.

Heaven would be no more
Than life we find on earth
If Jesus was not there
And we had not the new birth.

March 14, 1989

Right On Time

The last poem was "He'll Be There," and the next one is "Right On Time," written on March 14, 1989. I doubt that I remember the one when I wrote the other. I don't even know which was written first. They may have been written at a time I needed a faith builder, but I will never know for sure. It may also have been a time when someone else was in need of being encouraged and I was writing with them in mind.

When Moses came to the Red Sea
Old Pharaoh's army right behind
He knew he wouldn't have to worry
His God, he knew he'd find.

He'll be there always on time
Just rest your cares on Him
He'll be there at your side
Even when your vision's dim.

He's always taken care of us
We are one of His own
We can depend upon Him
Even when the way is unknown.

When old Daniel looked ahead
He saw the big old lion
He cried, "Oh, I thank my God
I know that he is mine."

As old Stephen was a dying
He looked up to the throne
There, he saw the savior standing
For he was one of His own.

March 14, 1989

What If He Did It Again

I often read the Bible and think of how different things are at times. Then again, they are not really different either. Before Jesus died on the cross, people didn't have the Grace that we are under now. We have the story in Acts, chapter 5, of the man and his wife who lied to the Spirit about the amount of money they got for the land they sold. I don't know if they are the only people who died for lying to the Spirit or not but, I have often wondered how people get by with what they seem to get by with. But, I have to remember, I don't know people's hearts and I have enough to do in keeping myself right before God.

You know the story well, how a man and his wife
Because they lied to the Spirit, were relieved of their life
What if God did it again, like He did in days of old?
How many of us would stand, or how many would be so bold?

Achan thought no one would know if the treasures he did hide
When sin was in the camp, God would not come inside
You know what became of him, and all his family, too
As the earth opened up, you know with him, God was through.

Date Unknown

The Year Of Ninety-Eight

The next poem was written on January 2, 1998. I knew my mother was not in good health, and I could have been wondering if she would leave us soon. There are lots of things I could have been wondering about in this poem. Some of the poems in this last section are short and I just found them laid aside.

Just entering the year of ninety-eight
Leaves me to wonder what it will hold
Will we see the things for which we wait
As before our dreams unfold.

Oh, year of many wonders, splendid
Grips our ever longing heart
Our farewells to earth we bid
As from this timely trial we depart.

We glory in the living Grace
Of God's most bountiful Love
Where someday we will take our place
In our glorious home above.

What do we long for on this earth?
Surely, not for fame or wealth
But only for that new birth
For others, as for our self.

Time is walking on the edge
Of that grand eternal day
Where the King of all ages
Takes His beloved, far away.

Far above the cares of life
Where sorrowful tears will never fall
Far beyond the reach of strife
Eagerly, we answer his call.

As He calls us from a world of sin
Into that glorious eternal land
As He welcomes His bride in
And places the band upon her hand.

Oh year of nineteen ninety-eight
May our dreams, you fulfill
As all the saints anticipate
The unfolding of God's will

January 2, 1998

Stand Up For Jesus

The next poem was written on March 14, 1989. I do not know what inspired me to write it, but I was probably tired of hearing about somebody protesting about something that was not important to me. The Christian is the only one that has something worth standing up for. We can stand up for Jesus, because He is always right. It seems that Christians are too quiet and need to let it be known whom they believe in and why.

Every day we see people are standing
For what they feel is their right
They are ready for a protest
Even ready for a fight.

What about us Christians?
Are we standing for our Lord?
Or do we take Satan's pushings
Never uttering a word?

Get on the team of Jesus
Stand up for what is right
Knowing where He wants you
Stand up with all your might.

The quiet people in our world
Are the children of God
We seem to have forgotten
Where the saints' feet have trod.

In the Bible, we are told
Of Shadrach, Meshach and Abednego
They would stand for the Lord
They told the old king so.

March 14, 1989

You Don't Have To Wait For Heaven

I must have really been in the mood to write on March 14, 1989 because this one is also written on that date. I know a lot of people would disagree with me about having heaven on earth. There are really times in this life when it seems we are in heaven, although we don't know what heaven is really like. Eyes have not seen, nor have ears heard what awaits us. When Jesus lives in your heart and is with you day and night, it is wonderful. I do know, we have problems, and it certainly doesn't seem like heaven. I also know there is a place in God that we can walk, and it seems like heaven, even though we don't walk there every day.

So many people are waiting and talking
About a great home over there
When they have crossed Jordan River
Where there will never be a care.

You don't have to wait for heaven
When Jesus lives in your heart
How much closer can He be?
Your heaven will then start.

It is joy unspeakable
And full of glory here
When we let Him have control
And live without a fear.

Jesus said, I will not leave you alone
For when I get back to my Father
I will pray to Him, your God
To send you another comforter."

While we dwell in this old world
We can have heaven within
Then one day, we'll be raptured
Far away from this world of sin.

March 14, 1989

If You Have A Light, Just Let It Shine

I didn't realize until I started putting this book together, that I had written at least eight poems on March 14, 1989. I don't know of any special event that happened on that day to inspire so many poems. I guess the next poem was my way of saying, "If you are a Christian, act like it. If you have a light of Christ, let others see it."

We often hear the children sing
"This Little Light of Mine"
Well, if you are a Christian
Just let your little light shine.

Where should we let it shine?
In the home it's needed most
Just let it shine, as you would
If Jesus were your host.

We often talk of a dark world
Where sin is all around
We don't seem to understand
We Christians must abound.

Maybe your little light is dim
Barely able to cast a glow
A little oil of the Spirit
Will make it bright as you know.

Your little light, my little light
Will make a brilliant beam
In the corner of our world
It won't be dark as it seems.

March 14, 1989

Songs We Love

I have had a lifetime of singing and hearing good singing. There are songs that I can never hear too often. The old songs are never old to me. The modern songs sometimes leave out the Blood of Jesus. Without the Blood, there is no Hope of Heaven. I have chosen some of the ones that I have heard all my life and tried to write a poem, using the titles. Another one that was written on March 14, 1989.

I love to hear the old songs the choir used to sing
They were filled with melody, making the heavens ring.

We sang Glory to the Lamb, When the Saints Go Marching In
How wonderful we felt, as we sang, Tell Me His Name Again.

Amazing Grace, how sweet the sound, seems older than the hills
Yet, every time I sing it, I feel the same glorious thrill.

How Beautiful Heaven Must Be, puts in mind a heavenly view
Of a clear crystal river flowing, by the throne of God, too.

This Is Just What Heaven Means To Me, I Firmly Promise You
I'll Meet You In The Morning, When We All Get To Heaven, too.

He'll Hold To My Hand, upon the Jericho Road
When I place my hand in His, He will help me carry the load.

Oh, I want to See Him, When We March Around the Throne
Oh, Happy Day, Hallelujah, and I'm glad I'm one of His own.

We Shall See The King, When the Saints Are Gathering In
I'll Thank Him, I'll Praise Him for saving my soul from sin.

Heaven's Jubilee, and There's Going To Be A Meeting In The Air
When The Roll Is Called Up Yonder, Look For Me, I'll Be There.

Nearer My God To Thee, oh, Blessed Jesus, Hold my Hand
Some glad morning I'll Fly Away, and Camp In Canaan's Land

March 14, 1989

For Such A Time As This

The book of Esther, in the Bible, is one of my favorites. The Jews are God's chosen people and you can believe He will take care of them. Esther found favor with the king, and was chosen to be the queen. She found favor with God, long before she was chosen queen. Mordicai told Queen Esther, "No doubt she had become queen, for such a time as this.

We never know what God has for us to do in His kingdom. We are placed in the world, at this End-Time, to fulfill a work for God. Ask God what He has for you to accomplish.

When Haman, seeking favor from the king
Sought to have the Jews killed
What he didn't really know
This could happen only if God willed.

Mordicai spoke to his royal cousin
Queen Esther was her name
He said, "Who knows but for this purpose
To the throne you came."

He requested she speak unto the king
Asking for her people a sparing
To go unto the king without being called
She knew was very daring.

Word was sent to Mordicai too fast
She and her court would fast also
Then, she would go before the king
Plans of Haman, he must know.

As always, fasting caught God's attention
Queen Easter went unto the king
Haman was hung upon his own noose
For planning all those evil things.

Be careful the evil you think
Or perhaps you devise
What you sow, you reap
Let all your ways be wise.

March 14, 1989

There Are No Heartaches

Another March 14 poem. I wish I could remember what was going on in my mind that day. I know it was only three months since my Daddy died and two month's since Woody's brother, Bill's death.

In the book of Revelation
In chapter twenty one, we find
God shall wipe all tears away
Leave not a worry in our mind.

There will be no more heartaches
There will be no sorrows there
We will live ever in splendor
There will never be a care.

Many times, we are faced with problems
Many times, we just weep and weep
There are times we are tossed
All through the night we can not sleep.

It hasn't entered the heart of man
We simply cannot imagine
What He has prepared there
Waiting for us to enter in.

March 14, 1989

Please Don't Ask Me To Be Still

I have been in Pentecostal churches all my life. I was a very quiet, shy child when I was growing up. But, in 1963, when God filled me with the Holy Ghost and fire as spoken of in the second chapter of the book of Acts, I have not been quiet or shy. I don't remember the reason for writing this poem. I don't know if I got the impression for praising the Lord from my heart. If you don't like shouting, don't go to heaven. If you don't like noise, don't go to hell. Those are the only two choices. So, learn to like one sound or the other.

On the Day of Pentecost
When one hundred twenty were filled
They could be heard all over town
None asked them to be still.

Please don't ask me to be still
There is no dead spirit in me
I shout and praise the Lord
Ever since He set me free.

Churches of this modern day
Have forgotten how it feels
When every fiber of their being
Would refuse to be still.

I came up the old time way
When the people were not afraid
To run and praise the Lord
As on the altar, their sins were laid.

Date Unknown

The Older Brother And Judas

I worked on a job where I was under the impression that if I learned the responsibilities of the secretary, I could move into her position when she retired. I worked hard and she had me trained well. I did a lot of her work, so I would know how, when the day came. Well, the day came and things didn't just happen like I thought they would. An ad was placed in the paper and opportunity given for people to apply other than myself. I was not the one to get the job, but I was to train the person who did get the job. She didn't know how to use the computer.

The person in charge told me that I acted like the older brother of the prodigal son. To me, he was acting like Judas who betrayed Jesus. That is how this poem came about and, no, I didn't stay and train her on the computer.

I'm not certain they ever met
The brother of the Prodigal son
And a man named Judas
He who betrayed the lowly one.

First, we'll examine the brother
I don't even know his name
He was so angry and upset
When home, the Prodigal came.

The father said, "Kill the fatted calf
Let all of us make merry"
My son was lost, but now is found
My life no longer will be dreary.

The older brother refused to be glad
He failed to see all he owned
He only knew he had been faithful
While the Prodigal had been gone.

Judas was a disciple of Jesus
Walked daily by His side
Seemingly the kind of person
Who flowed along with the tide

He carried the money bag
Seems money was his fall
For only thirty pieces of silver
He gave his soul and all.

He betrayed one he called a friend
Caused the Savior grief and pain
Instead of seeking forgiveness
He came not to Christ again.

How many betray with a kiss?
They hurt the ones who care
May they recall deceiving Judas
Noticing his eternal fare.

May 17, 1991

What Would They Say

I wrote this poem to enter in a contest in 1991. Only thing, I missed the deadline and never mailed it. I could have entered later, never did. I have no patience with people who don't love America and its Flag. People like this, make me think of a child, who would slap the hand of his mother, while she is feeding him. I never understood people being fed by the government, and burning the flag, the same day. Check it out and see the type of people who hate the flag.

Our courts grant the privilege
To walk on, and burn our Flag
Makes a person wonder
Were all those wars a gag?

To see her, brings tears to my eyes
When I think of where she has been
The millions who lie still and cold
I am sure they would fight again.

The Flag waves for our freedom
Her own, seemingly she has none
What would they burn in protest
If Old Glory had not won?

We have heard from the rebellious
Watched their destructive way
Those brave men at Iwo Jima
I wonder, what they would say.

Well, let me say it for them
And I will not spare any
If, you don't love freedom
Countries without it are plenty.

Freedom comes with a price
A lot are not willing to pay
Keep your thoughts to yourself.
You lost a right to a say.

1991

What Is Your Idol?

This is another of those poems written on March 14, 1989. Most of us have an idol, whether we know it or not, or whether we admit it or not. It is anything we give more of our devotion to, than God. Most of the time, we don't realize that we have idols. Because we don't spend time being devoted to God, we are prey for the enemy. Satan doesn't want us to see our faults, so he keeps us busy, busy, very busy.

In the book of Exodus, chapter twenty, you'll find
God gave to Moses Ten Commandments
Each was a very important guide
None of these rules were to be bent.

Thou shalt have no other god before me
The Bible so clearly said
Seeing the way people live today
I wonder if these commandments are read.

You may look all around
Just anywhere you may glance
You will see all the other gods
Leaving love for God to chance.

Look into your own life, please
What has first place with you?
Have you set some idol up
So, to God you are not true?

Where do you spend all your time?
What do you enjoy doing best?
If God is not foremost in your life
All of your idols won't stand the test.

Think of what you are doing
Before you find it is too late
When at last you try to enter
Your idol will block the pearly gate.

March 14, 1989

Let Not Your Heart Be Troubled

This poem was written on July 2, 1993, about a couple of weeks after my sister, Wanda died. I read in the Bible, John 14: 1-3, "Let not your heart be troubled: ye believe in God, believe also in me. In my Father's house are many mansions: if it were not so, I would have told you, I go to prepare a place for you, and if I go and prepare a place for you, I will come again, and receive you unto myself: that where I am, there ye may be also."

This is the promise we have from the Son
To take us when life's work is done
How can our hearts be troubled today?
Even though death took Wanda away.

A mansion He went away to prepare
After this life, we have no care
No more troubles, no more pain
When Heaven, our home, we gain.

Jesus is our eternal life
In Him there is no strife
What we place in His hands to keep
Will be there when we fall asleep.

Imagine a mansion of our own
There in worlds to us unknown
Where Jesus sits upon His throne
Our burdens are forever gone.

Each of us will have our call
To leave this earth and all
May we be able to hear Him say
"Come, I finished your mansion today."

What is life, but a vapor here
While death is ever lingering near
We have no surety pass today
Do not wait, for time to pray.

Pray now, while He is calling
Less to late you are falling
Into the depths of despair
Where hell does not care.

A mansion He will give
To all who learn to live
In the shelter of His wing
And daily, His praises sing.

July 2, 1993

Could We Find Room For Him?

December 3, 1994, I was getting another Newsletter ready to mail out to my family. This was my famous page four, where usually I had a poem. This was 10 days before my father-in-law passed away.

Quite often, I compare the people around me with those in the Bible. We can certainly point our fingers at the people we read about. But guess what? We are so much like the people in the Bible, it is almost strange. We like to think that all those evil people who crucified Jesus were the worst of sinners. How many times did we crucify him afresh this week? Had a little pregnant girl come to our home on Christmas Eve, would we spoil our Christmas to make her comfortable? Helping those who can't help themselves is what Christmas is all about. The real reason we have another holiday.

In Bethlehem, city of so long ago
Weary from searching for awhile
To find a room and place to sleep
For his wife great with child.

The city was crowded and loud
From people too busy with cares
The father moved on a space to find
Amid all the noise and stares.

Each inn was already filled
No one willing to move aside
Allowing a young mother-to-be
A place where she could abide.

In a lowly, stable of the inn
She brought forth her newborn son
As the crowds in splendor slept
Knowing not a new day had begun.

Suppose it was nineteen-ninety-four
And Jesus was looking for a place
Would it be easier now than then?
Where in this world would He find space?

The courts would try to rid him
Claiming, need not over populate
And use up all the goods of earth
That is how our babies meet their fate.

As to His Father should he bow his head
The whole school would be disgraced
The thought of some child praying
Won't happen in this place.

As the atheists have their way
He would be given sex education
At an early age in life
Until the time of graduation

He would be taught evolution
You know, how man came from monkey
How the earth got here with a bang?
Never understood for the life of me.

Could he even find a home
Filled with His Holy Way
Where he could learn the ways of God
And hear his parents really pray?

Could he stand the programs on TV
With all the evil and crime
Would he be taken to church
Or would his parents have no time?

Could He find a place in your home?
Would your friends, of Him be ashamed?
Would He acknowledge you before God?
Tell me, who is to blame?

December 3, 1994

Gabriel Has The Trumpet Ready

Not certain when I wrote this one, but it was somewhere between 1977 and 1979. Trish and I sang it sometime while we attended the Monticello Church of God. I couldn't play music, and we didn't have anyone to play for us. Actually, I can't write music, even though I can sing in the tune I write it for.

This poem is placed in here last because I really believe we are at the time the Bible tells us about. We are in the days just prior to the coming of Jesus. While I don't attempt to say the day, nor hour of his return, I can, based on the Bible, say we that love His appearing, and are ready, shall soon behold Him.

We hear it on the radio
See signs throughout the land,
That Jesus will soon return.
That day is now at hand.

Gabriel has the trumpet ready
It's polished and in tune
Just waiting for the day
I know it must be soon.

The trumpet will be sounding
Calling all the saints of God
First will come, the dead in Christ
Rising from the cold sod.

Look around you, brother
Are all the lost ones in?
Are you doing all you can
To pull the lost from sin?

What is the reason friend?
You seem to hesitate?
Don't you know you will be left?
If for too long, you wait?

Date Unknown

Printed in the United States
221076BV00001B/2/P